Steadfast *Spirit*

*Savoring a Lenten journey
to uncover spiritual 'finds' in real-time*

John Schroeder

STEADFAST SCRIVENER PRESS, LLC
Manchester, Missouri

www.withusstill.blog

Steadfast Spirit: Savoring a Lenten journey to uncover spiritual 'finds' in real-time

Copyright © 2020 by John Schroeder

Cover design: Gerri Schroeder
Cover photo: John Schroeder

Steadfast Scrivener Press, LLC
Manchester, MO

www.withusstill.blog

All rights reserved. This book or any portion thereof may not be reproduced or used in any manner whatsoever without the express written permission of the publisher except for the use of brief quotations in a book review.

First Edition

ISBN 978-1-79483-825-3

"Blog post" scripture texts in this work are taken from the *New American Bible, revised edition* © 2010, 1991, 1986, 1970 Confraternity of Christian Doctrine, Washington, D.C. and are used by permission of the copyright owner. All Rights Reserved. No part of the New American Bible may be reproduced in any form without permission in writing from the copyright owner.

"Ponder and pray" scripture taken from *The Message*. Copyright © 1993, 1994, 1995, 1996, 2000, 2001, 2002. Used by permission of NavPress Publishing Group.

Library of Congress Control Number: 2020900023

To Mary Geralyn,
my beloved spouse and muse

A clean heart create for me, O God,
and a steadfast spirit renew within me.
Cast me not out from your presence,
and your Holy Spirit take not from me.

Psalm 51: 12-13

Contents

Introduction: 'Found' Spirituality   1

Daily Lenten Reflections   5

Triduum & Easter Reflections   137

Introduction
Finding my way to 'found' spirituality

Does the Holy Spirit speak today?

More to the point: Can an admittedly imperfect disciple accurately detect whispers from the Holy One – whether regarding timeless mysteries, or the blessings to be found in everyday events?

It's no more preposterous, I suppose, than for Jesus to have risen from the dead some two-thousand-plus years ago. Or for Jesus to come again, to become truly present each day – body and soul, blood and divinity – in a scandalously insubstantial wafer of unleavened bread.

God writes straight with crooked lines, they say. And I discovered a bit of the truth in that statement a few years back, on *Mardis Gras*. "Fat Tuesday." The eve of Lent.

I remember feeling pretty crooked that day: Not looking forward to a guilt-laden 40 days of renewal stretching out ahead of me. Knowing how often in previous years I had frittered away the grace available in those 40 days. Knowing that my resolutions focused on self-denial would inevitably implode, and perhaps spectacularly.

Then, unexpectedly came the whisper, penetrating my spiritual gloom. *"Write a blog this Lent. Write what I give you."*

And that's pretty much how I stumbled upon "found" spirituality a few years back. The Spirit murmured, and I resolved to *listen*, for once. I resolved to *look*. I resolved to *share* what I discovered, via a digital platform I was barely competent to wield.

So: Does the Holy Spirit speak today?

I was delighted to discover almost daily evidence of this phenomenon during the holy season in question. Now, in a slightly different form, I am pleased to pass the evidence along to you.

JGS
Manchester, Missouri
January, 2020

Editing Note

After wrestling a bit with how much to tweak the spiritual "finds" I initially recorded, I ultimately decided to leave them in as original a state as practical. Hyperlinks have been removed, with the source material now appearing in footnotes.

Otherwise, the content remains largely as it first appeared in the blogosphere, following an almost-daily publication routine. While that makes for an imperfect journal of what's traditionally known as a 40-day season, it preserves the real-time rhythm I experienced then, even as it highlights some technical snarls that nearly derailed the project in its very earliest days. (See "**Day 4: The devil [at least for me] is in the details**," below.)

As an aid to personal prayer and reflection, I have added a brief scripture passage to the end of each day's blog entry. I chose *The Message*® version of the Bible for these passages because I find Eugene Peterson's translation so eye-opening and engaging.

Day 1

Today's find: Thoughts about why we "do" Lent.

The thoughts surfaced when a friend asked our after-Mass coffee klatch to help him answer the question posed by his brother. (Steve was received into the Catholic church a few years back; and his brother, an evangelical Protestant, was basically challenging the scriptural foundation for observing a season of self-denial or preparation each spring.)

"Where is that in the Bible?" Steve asked. "What's this Lent thing really all about?"

These days, I tend to find such questions energizing. As a cradle Catholic, I've been doing Lent for as long as I can remember – some 50+ years – usually out of a sense of obligation (because the Church told me to) or else acting on a malformed notion of grace.

Clearly, my personal history wouldn't be much help to Steve or his brother. But was there another way to answer the question? Could we find some common ground, in the teachings and actions of the Master?

And I told Steve that I thought the answer was "yes." Sure, we know that Jesus cautioned against performing "righteous deeds in order that people may see them." (Matthew 6:1) He acknowledged too that fasting and self-denial had its limitations: "Can the wedding guests mourn as long as the bridegroom is with them?" (Matthew 9:15)

But just as clearly, Jesus saw some value in the spiritual practices that have become closely identified with the Church's Lenten traditions: "The days will come when the bridegroom is taken away from them, and then they will fast."

More to the point, the Master[1] himself provided the model for Lent. Luke tells us that before Jesus began his public ministry, he "was led by the Spirit into the desert for forty days" and that he "ate nothing during those days." (Luke 4: 1-2)

As the beloved son of the Father, Jesus certainly didn't wander into the desert trying to prove his worthiness or trying to earn an extra measure of grace. So what, exactly, did he go into the wasteland to discover?

---

[1] A dear friend (one who provides an often-prophetic spiritual voice in my life) pointed out, in the early days of this blog, how *masculine* my God-language tends to be. Not just words like "Master", but also nouns such as "Lord" and "Father" (and plenty more gender-bearing titles and pronouns) pop up throughout. This is a hot-button issue for some – then and now. For others, it's an inconsequential concern. I found myself responding to the Spirit's gentle nudge (as noted in "Day 14"), and have been working ever since to expand my God-vocabulary.

The evangelist is not terribly specific on that point. But it's reasonable to conclude that Jesus learned something about trust in the Father's providence during those forty days. Freed from worldly distractions, he also probably gained some insights into the work he was being called to do.

So perhaps Lent has less to do with guilt and/or reparation than I've been inclined to believe all these years. Perhaps it's an invitation to follow the Master's lead – and do something new, something scary, something fruitful with my life.

– δδδ –

Scripture, to pray and ponder:

But there's also this, it's not too late – God's personal Message! "Come back to me and really mean it! Come fasting and weeping, sorry for your sins! Change your life, not just your clothes. Come back to God, your God."

Joel 2: 12-13

Day 2

Today's find: Saints among us

It's February 14: Valentine's Day — if not the quintessential "Hallmark holiday," then at least among 'em. And as I mused about the crass commercialization of romantic love on what presumably began as a feast day for a saint, I started to wonder a bit about the man himself.

Would St. Valentine be pleased with all the paper hearts, red roses and chocolate truffles? Or simply confused, as to how this folderol had come to be associated with his name and good works?

Turns out, that wouldn't be a simple question to answer since there are about a dozen different saints named Valentine[2] who have been commemorated in the Roman Catholic Church over the centuries.

That little nugget of church history brought to mind all the many saints who have blessed my own life over the years. This is risky business of course, declaring one's contemporaries saints. On the other hand, when you know someone who's died a happy death, fortified by the sacraments, shouldn't you be confident that he or she has indeed been welcomed into the heavenly banquet?

---

[2] Source: Catholic Online http://bit.ly/2N0N1Ow

And so today, I find myself remembering with gratitude the saints I've known, particularly in my parish community – people who have touched my heart and shown me how God's grace remains vibrant and effective all around me.

- *Stan M.,* who astonished me with his gift of hospitality – calling me by name, and making me feel for the first time like a full member in our suburban parish community of 10,000 Catholics.
- *Jeff O.,* a special athlete with a huge heart, a remarkable will and a winning smile.
- *Mary Anne G.,* a high school missionary, dying a servant's death in a country far from home.
- *Jack L.,* a greybeard 35 years my senior, who, using both the golf course and daily Mass as his classroom, taught me much about what it means to be a man.
- *Alice K.,* mischievous and witty, full of faith, despite the untold pains she'd experienced as a mother and wife.
- *Tom D.,* a successful car dealer who found his greatest joy late in life when he learned about grace and forgiveness – free for the asking.
- *Jim T., Paul W.* and *Steve P.,* ACTS Retreat teammates who knowingly chose to spend some of their last Saturdays on earth sharing fellowship with us – and in the process, helped us all to appreciate a pearl of great price.

- *Father Jim K.,* dear mentor and friend, teaching me until the end, walking the pilgrim's way, always finding the courage to keep going.

The Hallmark rack has no section with sentiments written for friends like these. I guess their kind of love – a really big, big love – just can't be captured in a greeting card.

– δδδ –

Scripture, to pray and ponder:

Then [Jesus] told them what they could expect for themselves: "Anyone who intends to come with me has to let me lead. You're not in the driver's seat – I am. Don't run from suffering; embrace it. Follow me and I'll show you how. Self-help is no help at all. Self-sacrifice is the way, my way, to finding yourself, your true self. What good would it do to get everything you want...and lose you, the real you?"

Luke 9: 23-25

Day 3

Today's find: A call to action, in communion

Some years ago, a priest acquaintance introduced me to a traditional prayer that deeply enriched my daily reception of the Eucharist.

> *Soul of Christ, sanctify me.*
> *Body of Christ, save me.*
> *Blood of Christ, inebriate me.*
> *Water from the side of Christ, wash me.*
> *Passion of Christ, strengthen me.*
> *O good Jesus, hear me.*
> *Within your wounds hide me.*
> *Separated from you, let me never be.*
> *From the evil one, protect me.*
> *At the hour of my death, call me.*
> *And close to you, bid me*
> *That with your saints, I may be*
> *praising you forever and ever.*
> *Amen.*

It has changed me, remembering to say the prayer after I return to the pew: I'm far less likely to treat the act of communion as routine; far more likely to meditate on just what is happening here – Jesus, in flesh and blood, becoming part of my own flesh and blood. Jesus, feeding me, providing food and drink for the journey.

And every verse, it seems, is necessary. Even at the start of the day, I often find myself in need of a deep cleansing, or of fortification, or simply wanting a warm and comforting hug.

Saying the *Anima Christi*[3] helps me to linger just a bit longer in Christ's presence, before his still, gentle voice is drowned out by the demands of the day.

But truth be told, I always feel just a bit guilty, a bit self-centered, when I repeat the prayer. After all, by the end of it, I've just said "me" or "I" a dozen different times. Surely Christ has bigger fish to fry than to focus on my often petty, neurotic needs.

Today, though, I noticed something important about the prayer – how at the end it calls me into communion: *"that with your saints I may be..."*

—

Jesus, you do give me the strength I ask for each day, don't you? Then you also gently remind me that it's not only for my benefit that the strength has been given.

You ask me to join hands, to link arms, with all those who have also been fed – so that together, we can make the gift of your presence more widely known in the world.

---

[3] Source: Our Catholic Prayers   http://bit.ly/2Wpq8Y0

– δδδ –

Scripture, to pray and ponder:

I know how bad I've been; my sins are staring me down. You're the One I've violated, and you've seen it all, seen the full extent of my evil. You have all the facts before you; whatever you decide about me is fair. I've been out of step with you for a long time, in the wrong since before I was born. What you're after is truth from the inside out. Enter me, then; conceive a new, true life. Soak me in your laundry and I'll come out clean, scrub me and I'll have a snow-white life.

Psalm 51: 3-9

Day 4

Today's find: The devil (at least for me) is in the details.

I've discovered something vexing over the past few days: *"free" ≠ "easy"*, at least not when it comes to blog publishing software tools.

In theory, I'm down with the idea that a spiritual blog would be a fruitful method of almsgiving for me this Lent.

In practice, this means stretching my digital skillset a bit, so that I can start doing what several friends[4] and relatives have been doing for years: Carve out a parking spot for my writing on the Web.

The choice of publishing tools (Blogspot vs. WordPress) presented an early obstacle. Having navigated those shoals, I took the plunge, opting for the promise of "powerful" by embracing the

---

[4] While I stopped writing entries for *Steadfast Spirit* in 2013, I still blog regularly about found spirituality. That's not true for the bloggers who first inspired me, but whose online journals are now on extended hiatus (e.g. http://bit.ly/32OXc9U and http://bit.ly/2JB6zqB) Nevertheless, I am fascinated by how these long-lost links might still serve the Holy Spirit's purposes today. Even without refreshed material, the blogs can bring a measure of timeless, anonymous beauty into the world, edifying anyone who might stumble upon them.

Steadfast Spirit

WordPress technology. And frankly, it's not going well. My steadfast spirit has been jolted by the myriad set-up options available, many with intimidating and strange-sounding names.

If you're reading this, it means I've muddled my way through, humbled considerably by the recognition that my digital skillset perhaps needed a bit more stretching than at first I realized.

After spending many hours over the course of three days in WordPress fits and starts, I was delighted to have an all-day commitment on Saturday – taking me out of town, to Bloomington, Illinois, for a Kairos Prison Ministry[5] training session (and therefore, far enough away from my iMac to temporarily relieve any neurotic guilt about getting my blog to go "live").

A hundred and ninety miles away from my iMac, yes.

Still, I found myself right back in a technological briar patch, tangling with Beelzubul, on Day 4 of Lent.

I'd programmed the GPS unit to take me and my three Kairos companions to 1210 Fell Street, site of our meeting at Christ The King Episcopal Church. But the Garmin lady clearly was mistaken when she announced *"arriving at destination"*: Nothing but houses

---

[5] I was fairly new to Kairos (http://bit.ly/2JzR6XK) in 2013. It has since yielded much spiritual fruit in my life, and often provides fodder for my blogging.

on *this* street – no steeples or parish halls anywhere to be seen.

We wandered about Bloomington a bit, trying to discover whether Fell Street might have both a "North" and a "South" range of addresses. (All four of us are men, so of course, we wouldn't *think* of stopping to ask for directions!) Then it occurred to one of us to check out a devilish little detail: Could the church actually be in Normal, Bloomington's twin city?

A few tweaks to the GPS unit, and we soon enough found our way to Christ The King. And there, within a minute or two, I encountered another profound spiritual challenge. The details are excruciatingly mind-numbing, but the essence was this: The Kairos head office was challenging us to build an effective state-wide hierarchy to lead and promote the growth of the volunteer ministry.

Alas, more devilish details: The thirty of us in the room had been drawn to the ministry by the chance to encounter Christ (in my case, while serving on retreat teams inside two different prisons since 2010).

This retreat work is a significant commitment in itself: forty hours spent in team formation meetings over the course of several months, plus fund-raising and cookie collections, not to mention the 80+ hours devoted to the actual weekend. And now, we were being told that more, much more, was needed to make the ministry thrive within the state of Illinois: More meetings, more paperwork, more planning, more documentation, more training, more discipline.

It sounded hard to me.

No, verging on *impossible*: I have already served for a couple of years in such administrative functions for the Kairos ministry at Menard. I know how difficult it is to fill the seats at the table, and get the meetings organized – in part, because there is typically no "carrot" of Christic encounter in such activities. Experience tells me that I'm more likely to meet the Prince of Darkness in this type of work: in the drudgery. The rejection. The bureaucracy. The failure.

But at some point Saturday, I recognized a *pattern* here: How often I *submit* to the devil I encounter in the dreary details of this (or any other part) of my life.

I realized, too, where I had eventually wound up after my misdirected start on this first Saturday of Lent: In the welcoming arms of Christ the King.

Perhaps it was a bit of divine encouragement for the steadfast spirit I am hoping to allow to emerge in me over the next 40 days…

– δδδ –

Scripture, to pray and ponder:

Your lives will begin to glow in the darkness, your shadowed lives will be bathed in sunlight. I will always show you where to go. I'll give you a full life in the emptiest of places – firm muscles, strong bones. You'll be like a well-watered garden, a gurgling spring that never runs dry.

Isaiah 58: 10-11

Day 5

Today's find: The power of confession

No, not *that* kind of confession: sacramental confession.

This kind:

> "If you confess with your mouth that Jesus is Lord and believe in your heart that God raised him from the dead, you will be saved."

When I heard this excerpt from Paul's letter to the Romans (10: 9) at Mass, I was reminded of what a difference it has made in my own life since I actually started to confess, out loud, that Jesus is Lord.

On some level, I guess I've always *believed* it: Baptized as an infant, schooled in the Baltimore Catechism, connected throughout my life to worshiping faith communities, I've spoken the words of the Creed hundreds, if not thousands, of times over the years (but always from the safety of the crowd in the pews).

That's not the same as *confessing*, though, at least not for me. When I have had the opportunity to witness to my faith, individually – whether in retreat talks, as a catechist, or just over a cup of coffee with a friend – something extraordinary always seems to happen.

My words become the *Word*, living and active. Jesus stirs from the grave of history and walks among us again.

Jesus is here, healing.

Jesus is here, feeding.

Jesus is here, loving and laughing.

It's certainly not the case that Jesus needs *me* to get this work of his done in the world. There are millions of others with whom he shares the same gift, the same promise, the same invitation to confess.

What a remarkable thing, though, that he *does* seem to see something of value in my witness. He doesn't mind my brokenness, or my tepidness. Somehow, he finds those imperfections useful to the kingdom he desires to build.

It's almost as if Jesus is saying he agrees with what the wry songwriter Leonard Cohen once observed. Cohen noted that there's a crack in *everything*. And it's how the *light* gets in.[6]

---

[6] "Anthem" by Leonard Cohen. Source: AZLyrics.com http://bit.ly/32fnk0L

– δδδ –

Scripture, to pray and ponder:

If one man's sin put crowds of people at the dead-end abyss of separation from God, just think what God's gift poured through one man, Jesus Christ, will do! There's no comparison between [Adam's] death-dealing sin and this generous, life-giving gift. The verdict on that one sin was the death sentence; the verdict on the many sins that followed was this wonderful life sentence.

Romans 5: 15-16

Day 6

Today's find: The mystery in seeds

Seeds are in the news[7] – soybean seeds. A farmer and a biotechnology giant are tangling over who "owns" the genetically-engineered germplasm[8] in a strain of biotech seeds after the harvest. Or to put the issue another way, can you really *patent* an item in nature that regenerates on its own?

The legal questions at stake in this dispute are far beyond my pay grade. But I found it intriguing what one lawyer said when asserting the company's position: "…to suggest that plants just grow themselves is preposterous."

That's really *not* such a preposterous idea to me. Nor to Jesus, for that matter. He uses the mysterious action of seeds to help us learn something about God, and how God often works in the world (Mark 4: 27):

> *This is how it is with the reign of God: A man scatters seed on the ground. He goes to bed and gets up*

---

[7] *St. Louis Post Dispatch*, 2/18/13   http://bit.ly/2WRy1Wx
[8] Germplasm, explains *SeedQuest.com*, is "living tissue from which new plants can be grown. It…contains the information for a species' genetic makeup, a valuable natural resource of plant diversity."   http://bit.ly/2JOIdJI

day after day. Through it all, the seed sprouts and grows, without his knowing how it happens.

We are called to cooperate then in preparing for the harvest, in building the kingdom. But on some level, when the real action occurs, it's entirely out of our hands. Our call, our duty, is to keep showing up: We go to bed and get up, day after day, and it may well be that we are never blessed with the particular harvest our heart desires.

Not getting what *we* want, though, is not the same as being ineffective. Even the things that seem like failures or disappointments in our lives may well have a purpose or an impact that is beyond our ability to see.

By stepping forward in faith, we embrace a profound mystery – one that is artfully expressed by the prophet Isaiah (55: 10-11) in today's first reading at Mass[9]:

> *[The Lord says:]*
> *Just as from the heavens*
> *the rain and snow come down*
> *And do not return there*
> *till they have watered the earth,*
> *making it fertile and fruitful,*
> *Giving seed to the one who sows*

---

[9] When these reflections were written in 2013, we heard readings from Lectionary Cycle 1 on weekdays; and Year C on Sundays.

and bread to the one who eats,
So shall my word be
that goes forth from my mouth;
It shall not return to me void,
but shall do my will,
achieving the end for which I sent it.

Thank you, Lord, for seeds and the bounty they provide. Thank you, too, for the mystery that seeds contain. Thank you for giving us a chance to hold a piece of your truth in our hands.

– δδδ –

Scripture, to pray and ponder:

[God says]: "Just as rain and snow descend from the skies and don't go back until they've watered the earth, doing their work of making things grow and blossom, producing seed for farmers and food for the hungry, so will the words that come out of my mouth not come back empty-handed. They'll do the work I sent them to do, they'll complete the assignment I gave them.

Isaiah 55: 10-11

Day 7

Today's find: Court awareness

My beloved Saint Louis University Billikens won a big game last night[10], and I had the chance to be among those in the sell-out crowd, thanks to the generosity of one of my best friends in life. As it happens, his seats are directly behind the visiting team's bench. Most games, that doesn't matter much, because few of the "away" teams who play the Billikens ever muster much of a crowd.

Last night's opponent, though, brought a sizeable contingent: several hundred VCU [Virginia Commonwealth University] fans, clad in black, and seated right next to us in Section 116. In the basketball scheme-of-things, this game really mattered to them (and to us) because at least for now, first place was at stake. And as the game wore on, I was struck by something kind of intriguing.

As we looked out onto the court, the two sets of fans were seeing the *exact same* events transpire. One group, clad in Billiken blue, often rose to their feet, stamping, clapping, cheering in delight. In contrast, the other group seemed positively morose: their daubers down,

---

[10] SLU beats No. 24-ranked Virginia Commonwealth 76-62 on Feb. 19, 2013. For more, here's a game story in the *St. Louis Post Dispatch:* http://bit.ly/2qlqnY2

their spirits crushed, by a performance that fell well below their expectations.

That got me thinking about how much our perspectives can influence our experience of a particular event or encounter. We set our standards, adjust our vision to look for a specific outcome, and in the process, become less able to see.

I wonder if this sort of myopia is what Jesus had in mind when, in today's Gospel reading (Luke 11: 29-32), he admonishes the crowd not to look for "signs."

He understands our human nature, and how we're likely to be drawn to the regal splendor of a King Solomon, or perhaps to dramatic gestures of penance and self-mortification like the people of Nineveh. Don't let your vision become so narrow, he seems to say, because *"there is something greater than Solomon here"* – in the person of Christ, in the example of his selfless love and in his gentle touch of forgiveness.

If Jesus had been a basketball coach, I suspect he would have emphasized "court awareness." He would encourage us to see our little corner of the world with fresh eyes. He'd want us to examine our expectations, and perhaps challenge our disappointments. But mostly, he'd want us to understand how important it is that we work together, to make his kingdom come.

– δδδ –

Scripture, to pray and ponder:

"Don't secretly hate your neighbor. If you have something against him, get it out into the open; otherwise you are an accomplice in his guilt. Don't seek revenge or carry a grudge against any of your people. Love your neighbor as yourself."

Leviticus 19: 17-18

Day 8

Today's find: Big sin. Really big sin.

Now that I've got your attention, a disclaimer: I'm not about to let you peek under the hood at my most grievous personal faults – not via the blogosphere, at any rate.

I have a different kettle of "big sin" in mind, stirred up by a couple of biographic notes I've encountered over the past couple of days – one profiling Peter Damian and the other featuring Claude Heithaus, SJ.

Almost a thousand years separates the two men: Peter Damian died in 1072, while Father Heithaus lived in the 20th century. But they had one important trait in common: Neither was afraid to confront systemic evil.

In Peter Damian's case, he[11] was taking on the church during a particularly corrupt time in its history, challenging other bishops to change their evil ways.

Father Heithaus[12] is best remembered for speaking out against racism, leading the effort to integrate Saint

---

[11] More about Peter Damian: http://bit.ly/34z3T4N
[12] This blog provides some background about Fr. Heithaus: http://bit.ly/2NE7g3A

Louis University in the mid-1940s (and making SLU a pioneer in the desegregation of higher education).

I never used to think much about such "big sins," precisely *because* they're big: Even if I recognize the evil in the system, what am I supposed to do about it? That started to change for me though when I was introduced to some of Pope John Paul II's notions about corporate sin. (That's "corporate" as in "body of believers."[13] He wasn't really referring to profiteering companies.)

The pope's teachings helped me realize that I *do* have some responsibility here. Or more precisely, that *we* have some responsibility, as members of the body of Christ. And while I certainly can't tackle all the evil in the world, that's not exactly what I am being *called* to do.

There's no way I'm going to be able to fix the societal ills that have turned the U.S. into an incarceration nation,[14] for example. But I *can* light a candle, by serving on Kairos teams. I can be Christ's arms or feet, if only for a few hours, for the men I encounter on the inside of the prison. (And while I'm there, I discover, much to my delight, that *they* can be Christ to *me*, too!)

---

[13] Learn more about the notion here: http://bit.ly/2CaTDU3
[14] The statistics are truly remarkable: The US incarcerates at a higher per-capita rate than any other country in the world. http://bit.ly/33hFQaj

We can all profit, I think, from spending at least some of our time this Lent reflecting on Big Sin, and asking for nudges from the Holy Spirit to show us which of those candles might be inscribed with our names.

True, taking on Big Sin can be a daunting task, and we need to be prepared for the rigors of the road. So let me leave you today with a quote from Peter Damian, offering an intriguing bit of advice on that subject. *"When you are going from one place to another, or on a journey,"* he says, *"let your lips continually ruminate something from the scriptures, grinding the psalms as in a mortar, so that they may ever give forth an odor of aromatic plants."*

— δδδ —

Scripture, to pray and ponder:

Jonah entered the city, went one day's walk and preached, "In forty days Nineveh will be smashed." The people of Nineveh listened, and trusted God. They proclaimed a citywide fast and dressed in burlap to show their repentance. Everyone did it — rich and poor, famous and obscure, leaders and followers.

Jonah 3: 4-5

Day 9

Today's find: Roses

When I started this blog, I had a notion of roses in mind.

I was familiar with St. Thérèse of Lisieux and her shower of roses,[15] sent as signs that our compassionate Father has heard our prayers. Indeed, both my wife Gerri and my daughter Ellen love to tell of the roses they have received when they've asked for St. Thérèse's intercession.

So while I didn't have a grand plan in mind when I started *Steadfast Spirit* last week, I figured, "What the heck? Launch the site, and maybe the good Lord will send a few 'roses' my way, too."

So far, so good: I haven't gone a day without receiving a rose of "found" spirituality to write about. Even better, I have come to a certain sense of peace about all those daily entries, stretching out unwritten before me: The blog will be what it will be, and I really don't have to sweat the details.

Roses are on my mind in a particular way *today*, though, because I have been asked to set aside some extra time in prayer for Ellen and her friend Grace as

---

[15] Read more about the saint known as "The Little Flower" here: http://bit.ly/2NH9YFq

they prepare themselves spiritually for their mission trip to Haiti in early March.[16]

Today is their "sending forth" retreat, led by Sister Rosa Cecilia Espiños, SSND. And one of the prayers I've been given to say in solidarity with them is from St. Thérèse herself.

I invite you to pray it along with me now:

> *May today there be peace within.*
> *May you trust God that you are exactly where you are meant to be.*
> *May you not forget the infinite possibilities that are born of faith.*
> *May you use those gifts that you have received, and pass on the love that has been given to you.*
> *May you be content knowing you are a child of God.*
> *Let this presence settle into your bones, and allow your soul the freedom to sing, dance, praise, and love.*
> *It is there for each and every one of us.*

A beautiful blessing prayer, eh? And whaddya know: It dropped into my lap like another "spiritual rose," courtesy of Ellen and Grace and their courageous *yes* in response to the invitation to make their mission trip.

---

[16] Their "mission trip blog," though inactive today, remains a thing of beauty: http://bit.ly/2PTNpAe

Steadfast Spirit

We do tend to ask for roses from the Lord, don't we? And it's a delight when He responds in some tangible way.

Still, sometimes we forget that spiritual roses can (and perhaps ought to) be a two-way street. We might well wonder: Is it not possible to use our gifts and talents as a way of sending a bouquet to the Lord – a bouquet fashioned, perhaps, through our own creativity or compassion?

– δδδ –

Scripture, to pray and ponder:

[Jesus said] "Don't bargain with God. Be direct. Ask for what you need."

Matthew 7: 7

Day 10

Today's find: He also serves who only types

I learned something intriguing today about a dear priest-friend of mine. Sent to Rome in 1959 for his philosophy and theology studies, he had a ringside seat for Vatican II.

Although I've known Father Jim Allen, OMI, for more than 40 years (he even concelebrated at our wedding), I don't ever recall him telling that tale.[17]

As for myself, I was tickled to read about the summer job he landed in 1963, between the first and second sessions of the Council. Through one of his Oblate connections, "not-yet-Fr." Jim was asked to do some typing for the Holy Office (now known as the Congregation for the Doctrine of the Faith).

That's right, typing.

You see, the bishops had been invited to send their comments and suggestions for some of the documents that had been discussed at the first session. It was Fr. Jim's job to type those comments onto mimeograph stencils[18] so that they could be

---

[17] You can find Fr. Jim's recollection of those heady days here: http://bit.ly/2pM9WnL
[18] What's a mimeograph, you ask?   http://bit.ly/2Nl0pNt

reproduced and distributed to all the appropriate reviewers.

It was grunt work, true. But the lowly task also had a patina of historical import to it. As Fr. Jim puts it, "I knew that even the Holy Father might read what I was typing." It was important to get it right, too: to type those comments accurately even though "they were in Latin and a lot of it was repetitive."

I don't doubt that Fr. Jim handled the job with aplomb. He's an extraordinarily good touch-typist. I remember watching in awe as his fingers flew across the keyboard of the IBM Selectric in his office at St. Henry's Prep, where I went to high school in the early 1970s.

Still, reading about this Vatican II footnote to his life reminded me of a story I'd heard from another friend, an historical theologian. It seems that in the early 20th century, scholars discovered a scribal error in the *Rule of St. Benedict*[19] dating back to the eighth century. Instead of transcribing *conversatio morum* (way of life), as Benedict had intended, the copyist had written *conversio morum* (conversion of life).

Both terms have their usefulness in forming one's spirituality. But my theologian friend says that the

---

[19] A true spiritual classic written in the 6th century, the *Rule* is still in use today at monasteries around the world: http://bit.ly/2NP1QT9

discovery of the error has been an occasion for modern day Benedictine monks to revisit the significance of this ancient vow, and to deepen their appreciation of their calling.[20]

As a Lenten insight, I'd say the lesson is that little things really do matter. And we "choose the better part" (Luke 10: 42) when we do even the most menial tasks with great love and attention.

– δδδ –

Scripture, to pray and ponder:

Martha was pulled away [from Jesus] by all she had to do in the kitchen. Later, she stepped in, interrupting them. "Master, don't you care that my sister has abandoned the kitchen to me? Tell her to lend me a hand."

Luke 10: 40

---

[20] In his book *Your Grown-up Faith*, my theologian friend wrote about the implications of the scribal error on one's spirituality. It's available here: https://amzn.to/2qpa9xg

Day 11

Today's find: 'Seeing' and 'believing'

I heard an intriguing question at my ACTS team meeting[21] on Saturday morning. As is our custom, the team members were breaking open the word and reflecting on the scripture passages we'd be hearing at Mass on Sunday morning.

The Gospel, in this case, is the familiar account of the transfiguration – this year[22], Luke's version. (Luke 9: 28-36) Afterwards, in his reflection, our team's spiritual companion asked something along these lines: *"How did the apostles know that it was Moses and Elijah standing on either side of Jesus?"* I made a smart-aleck remark in reply, saying they'd probably seen their statues at the Temple. But I knew our leader had a point: Moses and Elijah both lived long before cameras had come onto the scene, so what made their faces recognizable?

"Seeing" was already on my mind with respect to this thought-provoking Gospel episode, thanks to a

---

[21] Parish-based ACTS Retreats have been a great blessing in my life, as they have been for tens of thousands of others over the past 25+ years. Read more about this lay-led Catholic apostolate here: http://bit.ly/2NnwaWk

[22] When these reflections were written in 2013, we heard readings from Lectionary Year C on Sundays.

Sunday reflection sent my way from the School Sisters of Notre Dame.[23]

The reflection featured a photo of a drop-dead gorgeous sunset; and yet, somewhat surprisingly, its call-to-action focused on a different one of the five senses entirely: *"How is God calling me to listen to what others are saying to me?"*

This is a key reminder, it seems to me: We shouldn't be tempted to dwell on the bright lights and pretty colors. The call is to *listen*.

Not that we're any different than Peter, James and John in that regard. Their first instinct is to erect a tent, extend the moment, maybe even sell a few tickets to the spectacle unfolding right before their eyes.

But notice what happens next: They are immediately enveloped in a cloud, making it *impossible* for them to rely on their sight any longer in that moment.

Teach me, Lord, when my senses fail, to become more comfortable with unknowing. Heal me of the desire to withhold belief until I have seen something for myself. Open my ears to listen for your voice, and to cherish the mystery I find in you.

---

[23] Find prayer resources offered by one province of the School Sisters of Notre Dame here: http://bit.ly/2CkoIEW

– ᪣ –

Scripture, to pray and ponder:

[Jesus said] "You're familiar with the old written law, 'Love your friend,' and its unwritten companion, 'Hate your enemy.' I'm challenging that. I'm telling you to love your enemies. Let them bring out the best in you, not the worst. When someone gives you a hard time, respond with the energies of prayer, for then you are working out of your true selves, your God-created selves. This is what God does. He gives his best – the sun to warm and the rain to nourish – to everyone, regardless: the good and bad, the nice and nasty."

Matthew 5: 43-45

Day 12

Today's find: A good measure

At Mass this morning, we heard one of my favorite passages from the Gospel according the Luke (6: 38):

> *"Give and gifts will be given to you; a good measure, packed together, shaken down and overflowing, will be poured into your lap. For the measure with which you measure will in turn be measured out to you."*

I love meditating on these words…

…because I can just imagine the scene when Jesus first said them, walking along the streets of Jerusalem with his disciples in tow, when they come upon the farmer's market. And just there, he sees it: a perfect example of what he's trying to teach them about God's love. "Look at that flour merchant in the corner stall, how *generous* he is with his customer! He's giving her every bit of her money's worth, and *more!*"

It's like Jesus is saying we can (and should) expect our heavenly Father to delight us. He is a "baker's dozen" God. A God of infinite goodness and bounty.

It reminds me of a bit of wisdom I heard on retreat a few years back. The director made an excellent observation about how oddly the principles of measures and mathematics work, when we willingly share fellowship with another member of the body of Christ. "God's economics," he called it: When you share a joy with another, it's *doubled*. When you share a burden, it's cut in *half*.

Don't know about you, but that's a system of weights and measures I can live with!

– δδδ –

Scripture, to pray and ponder:

[God] saved us and then called us to this holy work. We had nothing to do with it. It was all his idea, a gift prepared for us in Jesus long before we knew anything about it.

2 Timothy 1: 9

Day 13

Today's find: Sparrows

Yesterday was "laundry day" at our house, and in the late winter months, that means adding an extra step to the dreary routine. Along with sorting, soaping and spin drying, I also have to make a short trip outside – trudging through the snow and mud to remove the duct tape from the dryer vent opening on the exterior of our home.

You see, there's this sparrow who thinks the dryer vent hose would make a *dandy* place for a nest. And since sparrow nests and hot air don't mix, something's gotta give. So as soon as I hear the tell-tale scritching in the laundry room each February, I seal the opening as best I can, to encourage the bird to build elsewhere. (Is it the same sparrow year after year? Possibly, but not likely. Wild sparrows typically live for just three years or so, and this little duct-tape dance of ours has been going on for a decade or more. Who knows? Maybe they pass along my address from generation to generation. Or perhaps there's a "sparrow time-share" website that all the little birdies are connected to.)

Now I can't honestly say that I enjoy this whole bird-prevention process. Truth be told, it's kind of a pain in the kiester. But this morning, I happened across the words of Psalm 84 during my morning prayer:

> *My soul is longing and yearning for the courts of the Lord.*
> *My heart and flesh cry out to the living God.*
> *Even the sparrow finds a home,*
> *and the swallow a nest for herself*
> *in which she sets her young at your altars,*
> *O Lord of hosts, my king and my God.*

So, yes, I had to pause for a moment and confess that my life has been blessed by sparrows, by the prodigal beauty of nature – and by the way God seems to provide for even his most insignificant creatures.

As I read on in Psalm 84, I also noticed something else that seemed significant:

> *Blessed the people whose strength is in you, whose heart is set on pilgrim ways.*

That word *pilgrim* bears more reflection, it seems to me. It's clearly a part of what God calls us to be: people of the Way, always on a *journey*.

How often do I short-circuit that instinct in my own life, by clinging to possessions, or preferring the established habits and patterns in my life?

I've already turned one family of sparrows into pilgrims this spring. Perhaps through the words of Psalm 84, I'm being given a chance to follow their lead.

Steadfast Spirit

– δδδ –

Scripture, to pray and ponder:

Give groaning prisoners a hearing; pardon those on death row from their doom — You can do it! Then we, Your people, the ones You love and care for, will thank You over and over and over. We'll tell everyone we meet how wonderful You are, how praiseworthy You are!

Psalm 79: 11, 13

Day 14

Today's find: Abba

Vacation videos: They're not for the faint of heart. But every once in a while, a real gem emerges – as was the case a few years ago, when my brother-in-law was showing us clips from his trip to the Holy Land.

He had happened upon a playground in Jerusalem, packed with four- and five-year-olds clambering on a jungle gym – many of them, bleating for attention for their feats of derring-do: *"Abba! Abba! Abba!"* the kids would shout.

And that's when it hit me, just how badly translated this Aramaic word often is in our English versions of the Bible: Typically, the phrase is rendered (Mark 14: 36, Romans 8: 15, Galatians 4: 6) as *"Abba*, Father". But *Daddy* is probably more accurate.

It's as if it *shocks* us to think that Jesus was on such familiar terms with God – shocks us so much that we tend to add a layer of formality to the translation: *Father.*

Since seeing my brother-in-law's video, I've grown to love Jesus' term of endearment: *Abba*. My affection for it may have something to do with the fact that my own father died when I was 27, at a time when I was just learning to be a Daddy myself.

I needed an *Abba* then, and still do today, so I am grateful that Jesus gives me permission to call God "Daddy." I am grateful, too, for the holy men in my parish and in my prayer circles who have served *in loco parentis*, becoming important *Abba* figures for me over the years.

I am also aware that the term is *limiting* in a significant way. God is much bigger than my own projected needs, or than my own personal relationship with the Lord.

Yes, God *is* "Father."

God *is* "Daddy."

God *is* "*Abba.*"

God is also much, much more.

There's a moment during every Kairos Prison Ministry Weekend that brings this awareness into sharp focus for me. It happens on Sunday morning, when we lead our Kairos brothers through a meditation called "The Healing of Memories." It's a long prayer (much too long to reproduce here) but early on, there's a section in which the participants are asked to seek the Lord's help in freeing them from the hurts, the violence, the abandonment they may have experienced at the hands of their fathers. The implication is clear: When, as children, many of our incarcerated brothers called on "Daddy", the responses they received did anything *but* draw them into a loving relationship with God.

So why is *"Abba"* on my mind and in my heart today? Because a dear friend and I were chatting about this blog last evening. In the course of the conversation, she mentioned that she noticed how often I use masculine pronouns to refer to God.

Now, that seems natural enough to me: God, Father, *Abba:* Wouldn't it be appropriate to also refer to the Lord as "he" in second references?

On the other hand, God has given me talents as a writer, one of which is to seek *precision* in the words I choose. So if I want my writing to draw myself (and others) closer to the Lord, can I really afford to keep *all* my references to the Mighty One gender-specific?

I'm not sure if I'm quite ready to abandon masculine pronouns completely in my blogging about spirituality. But perhaps like any good *Abba,* God is gently encouraging me (through my friend's observation) to expand my horizons a bit during this holy season. Perhaps I am being invited to grow in my relationship with the great I AM: The One who is *God, Beyond All Names.*[24]

---

[24] This is the title to one of my favorite hymns, written by Bernadette Farrell – and performed by her here: http://bit.ly/32ncTIH

– δδδ –

Scripture, to pray and ponder:

[The Pharisees] love to sit at the head table at church dinners, basking in the most prominent positions, preening in the radiance of public flattery, receiving honorary degrees, and getting called 'Doctor' and 'Reverend.' Don't let people do that to you, put you on a pedestal like that. You all have a single Teacher, and you are all classmates. Don't set people up as experts over your life, letting them tell you what to do. Save that authority for God; let God tell you what to do.

No one else should carry the title of 'Father'; you have only one Father, in heaven. And don't let people maneuver you into taking charge of them. There is only one Life-Leader for you and them – Christ. Do you want to stand out? Then step down. Be a servant. If you puff yourself up, you'll get the wind knocked out of you. But if you're content to simply be yourself, your life will count for plenty.

Matthew 23: 6-12

Day 15

Today's find: Benedict Emeritus

Along with the world's 1.2 billion Roman Catholics, I witnessed a remarkable event today[25]: Pope Benedict XVI retired from the papacy, the first pontiff to do so in about 600 years.

My heart is deeply grateful for his service to the church. To my mind, it's made all the more remarkable for his having taken on a very difficult responsibility at an age when most people have already been retired for years. And in some respects, that initial "yes" of his papacy pales in comparison to this final act of selflessness. I see Christ in Pope Benedict and in his diminishment today. I am blessed by the particular way he now demonstrates his love for the church.

At the same time, this pontificate leaves me a little heartbroken, too. I was troubled to read in recent months about the vicious in-fighting in the Vatican – the power struggles and dissension that may well have played a role in Pope Benedict's decision to retire.

It shouldn't surprise me, I suppose, that there's jockeying for position even within the Curia. As we saw in yesterday's reading from Matthew's Gospel (20:

---

[25] February 28, 2013.

17-28), power plays have been a part of our sinful church from the very beginning.

My own "patron saint" John and his brother James bore the brunt of the ignominy in that memorable episode – as they sought, with an assist from their mother, seats of prominence on either side of Jesus. But Matthew assures us there were no clean consciences among the rest of the Apostles: "When the ten heard this, they became indignant at the two brothers."

We never seem to get this part of discipleship right, do we? (We men, anyway.) The chatter lately has been all about whether the Pope Emeritus will continue to wear red shoes,[26] a traditional sign of the office.

What Jesus tried to show us is that it's more important that we learn how to wash feet. (John 13: 1-17)

Ignore that call from our Lord, and it won't be long before egos take over, and the power struggles begin. So as we pray in gratitude for Pope Benedict today, let's pray for ourselves, too.

Let's pray for the holy, broken men in the College of Cardinals who will be gathering soon to elect a successor. And let's pray that each of us becomes more faithful to Jesus' call, asking that we be given

---

[26] Seriously? Aren't there more important things for the men in Rome to be thinking about?   https://wapo.st/2JVwTvG

servants' hearts, along with the grace to resist the allure of power and prominence.[27]

– δδδ –

Scripture, to pray and ponder:

Don't you know anything? Haven't you been listening? God doesn't come and go. God lasts. [God is] Creator of all you can see or imagine. He doesn't get tired out, doesn't pause to catch [a] breath. And he knows everything, inside and out. [God] energizes those who get tired, gives fresh strength to dropouts. For even young people tire and drop out, young folk in their prime stumble and fall. But those who wait upon God get fresh strength. They spread their wings and soar like eagles. They run and don't get tired, they walk and don't lag behind.

Isaiah 40: 28-31

---

[27] The successor they elected, of course, is Pope Francis. From the earliest days of his papacy, he's made it a point to refuse many of the perks of office. So I guess you could say this prayer I made in 2013 has certainly been answered – all thanks and praise to You, Holy Spirit!

Day 16

Today's find: Re-JECT-ion!

"Not in *my* house!" That's what the seven Catholic universities of Big East fame[28] seem to be saying to my beloved Saint Louis University Billikens.

The "Catholic 7" are about to launch (or perhaps more accurately, re-launch) a big-time college basketball conference. And they need a few more like-minded universities to round out their league.

Now, I can give you a dozen good reasons why the Billikens would make a great addition to the conference – only 10 or 11 of which are completely self-interested, from a SLU fan's perspective. But at least for the moment, it looks like two other fine schools (Xavier and Butler) are going to get the nod instead.

And "True Confessions" time: I didn't exactly take it well when I saw that little tidbit scroll across ESPN's college b-ball broadcast last night.

In fact, I became slightly unhinged, reflexively hurling a few salty epithets at the flat-screen. *(I'm ever-so-sorry my dear wife Gerri had to hear all that!)*

---

[28] The snub still smarts my "Billiken fan" heart, because I *know* we can play with these guys: http://bit.ly/33AkQeM

No doubt, you're thinking: Get a grip, Big Fella. This is only college basketball we're talking about here. And I admit: I tend to take such things *way* too seriously.

But that's not the only defect of character that caught my attention after I finished spewing venom in the wake of the disappointing news about the Billikens. I noticed an all-too-familiar pattern of reaction in response to rejection.

Push one of my hot-buttons, and almost instantaneously I become defensive. Judgmental. Sarcastic. Petty. All that, before spiraling into the gaping maw of self-pity. Often, my instinct is to lash back: to hurt *them* for hurting *me*. Which, when I think about it, is like the spiritual equivalent of an offensive foul in basketball.

So maybe "court awareness"[29] isn't the only lesson I am supposed to learn about holiness from the hardcourt this Lent. It's Friday, after all: A good day to contemplate how different my reactions are, compared to those that Jesus displayed on the way to the cross on Good Friday.

Remarkably, the deep disappointments and cruel words he experienced that day did not seem to stir up bitterness in him. Jesus willingly shouldered even the

---

[29] See 'Day 7' above.

gravest injustice, and met all manner of insults and indignities with compassion and forgiveness.

—

How far my heart is from embracing the wisdom and power of your gentle way, dear Lord!

Teach me to love as you love! Break the chains that bind me to old habits of thinking and acting. Help me not to dwell on the pains I encounter in life, but aided by your grace, to pick-and-roll[30] right past 'em.

– δδδ –

Scripture, to pray and ponder:

God's Message: "Cursed is the strong one who depends on mere humans, who thinks he can make it on muscle alone and sets God aside as dead weight. He's like a tumbleweed on the prairie, out of touch with the good earth. He lives rootless and aimless in a land where nothing grows. But blessed is the man who trusts me, God, the woman who sticks with God."

Jeremiah 17: 5-7

---

[30] Great offenses frequently feature this classic basketball move: http://bit.ly/2NLFRgb

Day 17

Today's find: Presence

One of my unofficial tasks on the Men's ACTS team this spring is "deejay": Our Spiritual Companion has asked me to play a centering song at our formation meetings each week, just before we break open the scripture and then listen to his reflection.

I love the job.

I love it, in part, because it's a great opportunity for "found" spirituality. There's a fairly extensive collection of God-centered tunes on my iPod: 600 songs or so, out of the 4,700 total tracks. (Most of the rest is rock/pop, country, jazz or alternative – with some "classical" favorites mixed in, too, in case you're wondering.)

Blessed with this bounty of 600 songs, I'm never quite sure what kind of nudges I'm going to receive from the Holy Spirit. "What's going to be on the playlist this week?" But I typically start the selection process with scripture – specifically, the readings we are scheduled to hear at Mass on Sunday morning.

So being the team's deejay is kinda like a double-bonus for me: I get to search through a library of songs I love. And I get a head start on preparing my mind and heart for the Sunday liturgy.

Which brings me to the topic of today's blog entry: *Presence*. (You probably thought I'd never get there, didn't you? Apologies for the long-winded set-up!)

I'm tuned into *Presence* today, because of the story we hear from the book of Exodus tomorrow at Mass: Moses, and his encounter with the burning bush. (Exodus 3: 1-15)

Most of us have heard the story many times before. So often, that we tend to rush right past the remarkable exchange that's taking place there. Through Moses, we are told what we are to *call* God, how we will *know* God: "I AM."

It's not really a name, is it? It's a reassurance. It's a promise. "God is present. All is well." And that's true, even if you have no idea what to make of the scene unfolding before your very eyes: a bush on fire, say, that isn't being consumed by the flames.

So we might all do well to take that promise with us, as we reflect on the story we hear about Moses.

Don't let that scene rush past.

Spend some time in *Presence*.

Know that wherever you are, you are on holy ground.

– δδδ –

Scripture, to pray and ponder:

Moses answered God, "But why me? What makes you think that I could ever go to Pharaoh and lead the children of Israel out of Egypt?" "I'll be with you," God said. "And this will be the proof that I am the one who sent you: When you have brought my people out of Egypt, you will worship God right here at this very mountain." Then Moses said to God, "Suppose I go to the People of Israel and I tell them, 'The God of your fathers sent me to you'; and they ask me, 'What is his name?' What do I tell them?" God said to Moses, "I-AM-WHO-I-AM. Tell the People of Israel, 'I-AM sent me to you.'"

Exodus 3: 11-14

Day 18

Today's find: Presence, Part 2

Mmmm: lemon meringue pie!

I had no idea that Mom was going to whip up my all-time favorite dessert in honor of my drop-in visit late Saturday afternoon.

Actually, I was on a bit of a mission, wanting to borrow her lopping shears for some deep pruning I'm planning to do.

Even when I'm intent on my own agenda, though, Mom still knows how to get my attention. That pie of hers is world-class, and virtually every other version I've tasted falls short of the standard she has set. (I mean, really: Who needs eight or nine inches of meringue piled on top of the delicious lemony custard? Enough already!)

It turned out that the take-home dessert wasn't the only surprise in store. My eldest brother Gerard was also home, so the three of us had a chance to chat for a spell. The topics ranged widely, but they all had a spiritual flavor to them, in part, because I was telling them for the first time about this Lenten blog (neither goes "online", so there wasn't much point in bringing it up earlier).

We talked some about the challenges of holiness, and how the key patterns of sinfulness in our lives seem to *accentuate* those challenges. We talked about how hard it often is to know God's will, particularly when we are navigating through significant pain and disappointment. (Gerard's own fidelity has long been an inspiration for me. He has suffered with bipolar disorder for most of his adult life – a condition which, among other things, has short-circuited a deep longing of his heart, to be ordained a priest. His illness is a constant source of frustration for him, and yet he remains one of the most prayerful men I've ever known.)

While it's safe to say that an exploration of holiness was *not* on my "to-do" list yesterday afternoon, the conversation wound up being a wonderful and unexpected gift. And when it came time to leave, it felt perfectly appropriate for Gerard to suggest that we close our time together with prayer.

Now, Gerard's a little "old-school" in that regard. He started rattling off the Lord's Prayer and was already to the fourth or fifth line before I could cross the room and join my hands to theirs.

"Let's say it like we mean it," I suggested to my big brother.

And so, we began again, slowly and meditatively. And for the second time in about seven hours on Saturday, I was struck by an almost palpable sense of Presence.

The family room at my mother's house, the house where we'd grown up, had unexpectedly become holy ground.

It's impossible to recreate the moment here. My words are wholly inadequate to the task. But let me attempt to sketch a vignette, by describing how some all-too-familiar words suddenly took on a much deeper meaning.

...hallowed be your name... (Yes, Lord: 'Hallowed!' 'Hallowed!' Let me linger in your name...your generous reassurance...your great 'I AM'!)

...your will be done... (If I pray it quickly, Lord, it's for cause: so often, I'm not sure I really mean it!)

...give us this day our daily bread... (Thank you, Lord! You have answered this prayer in my life now for 20,000 consecutive days. Why do I so often fret that tomorrow is going to be different?)

...as we forgive those... (This is often the hardest part, isn't it, Lord? Particularly forgiving those who know best how to hurt us deeply. Give me the grace, Lord, to forgive. Release me from the grudges and resentments I hold so dear!)

...deliver us from evil... (You are gentle, Lord – and quiet. So often, your voice is drowned out by the cacophony in life – the Evil One's signature sound. Remind me to slow down, and listen...really listen...for your Presence.)

It was for me an *Amen* moment, the chance to pray that prayer, and feel the Lord's Presence in the company of my mother and brother.

I don't think they'll mind my attempt to share the moment with the rest of you, via the blogosphere. (But the lemon meringue pie, *that* I'm keeping for myself!)

– δδδ –

Scripture, to pray and ponder:

Where is the god who can compare with You – wiping the slate clean of guilt, turning a blind eye, a deaf ear, to the past sins of Your purged and precious people? You don't nurse Your anger and don't stay angry long, for mercy is Your specialty. That's what You love most. And compassion is on its way to us. You'll stamp out our wrongdoing. You'll sink our sins to the bottom of the ocean.

Micah 7: 18-19

Day 19

Today's find: Lopping shears

Today, I have pruning on my mind. With the "spring-forward" time change set for this weekend, I'm guessing the "spring thaw" won't be far behind. Sap soon will be rising, so it's now or never (this year, anyway) if I'm going to get the front landscaping back under control.

To prepare for the task, I borrowed a pair of lopping shears from my mother recently. And I almost can't wait to put those bad-boys into action. They look like a real he-man tool, with their jet-black 29" carbon-fiber handles and an exclusive "Power Lever" design that lets you cut "2X easier," according to the decal near the grip.

Now I know myself well enough to become suspicious whenever this sort of over-the-top energy starts to well up inside. Usually, it means I'm setting myself up for failure as I *leap* before I *look completely* into a project – one that turns out to be a bit more complicated than it first appears.

In this case, I've already asked for assistance from a landscaping professional. And while I'm waiting for a slot to open up in his schedule, I've had a chance to consider the spiritual implications of pruning.

Jesus himself calls it an important element of spirituality: God prunes *every* branch, he says – cutting *away* the ones that don't bear fruit, and cutting *back* the ones that do, so that they bear *more* fruit. (John 15: 1-6)

Look outside my front door, and you'll see an object lesson in the importance of deep pruning. There are yew bushes on either side of the front walk. Both shrubs are a deep, healthy green and are neatly trimmed into symmetrical cylinders. But after 20 years of growth, they're overhanging sidewalk now, turning a 36-inch wide path into just a 24-inch opening.[31]

Healthy bushes are a good thing, right? But in this case, they are limiting the ability of *other* good things to get in. Those yews definitely need some deep pruning.

Which is not unlike some of my own habits. Take TV viewing, for example. It's not a bad thing in itself. But it's become *way* too much of a time-waster in my life. Almost without fail, I pop the set on right after dinner. If there are no meetings on my evening schedule, it's not unusual for me to spend the next three or four hours under its spell.

---

[31] To see a photo of just how overgrown our yews had become, go online to view the original blog post: http://bit.ly/32plnPm

Last night, though, my wife Gerri beat me to the remote and suggested that we keep the TV dark for a while.

What a great idea! It gave me a chance to finish reading a book I'd been working on since last summer: Valerie Martin's *Salvation*, a novelized version of the life of St. Francis.

A day later, I don't know if I'm fully prepared to take a lopping shears to my TV viewing habits. But through Gerri's suggestion, the Lord seems to have put a pretty powerful tool in my hands.

Time, perhaps, for some deep pruning in this corner of my garden?

– 888 –

Scripture, to pray and ponder:

The [Samaritan] woman took the hint and left. In her confusion she left her water pot. Back in the village she told the people, "Come see a man who knew all about the things I did, who knows me inside and out. Do you think this could be the Messiah?" And they went out to see for themselves.

John 4: 28-30

Day 20

Today's find: Dave Brubeck

Dave Brubeck has been my boon companion throughout this Lent. Which is quite a trick, seeing as how the great jazz pianist died early last December.[32]

I've been hearing Dave's music just about every day, though, as I complete my 30-minute routine on the treadmill: One composition of his in particular, entitled *Forty Days*. I'm actually listening to two versions of it, one recorded "live",[33] the other, in studio (with his sons[34] accompanying him).

Like virtually all of Dave's music, this song has no lyrics, so I am left to interpret its notes, its rhythms and its movements on my own.

As I enter in to *Forty Days*, I am struck by a couple of things:

- First, how *different* the two versions sound to my ear. It's almost like hearing the same Gospel story (Luke 5: 1-11) told by two different

---

[32] Read a tribute to the great jazz man's accomplishments here: http://bit.ly/2PUvN7g
[33] From the album *'London Flat, London Sharp'* http://bit.ly/2JRgpoj
[34] From the album *'Two Generations of Brubeck'* http://bit.ly/2NkPZxc

evangelists (John 21: 4-8): There are familiar themes, sure. But important differences, too. And you really need to hear *both* in order to grasp the full truth.

- Second, how *energetic* the music is. In that regard, Dave's *Forty Days* provides a worthy challenge to some of my notions about Lent. I'm inclined to embrace a sackcloth approach to this holy season – to make it all about deprivation, sorrow and remorse. Dave's music takes me to a different place. It's almost like I can see *Jesus* "doing Lent," driven by the Spirit into the desert, the God-man on a mission. (Luke 4: 1-2) And though it's hard to keep pace, the invitation is there: *"Follow me. Come, take a hike with me!"*

I've long felt a connection to Dave Brubeck's music, precisely because of songs like *Forty Days*. He was a commercial success, one who made a living through his God-given talent. And from time to time, he just couldn't help letting his spirituality bubble up (and out) in his work.[35] He bridged the gap with his music, just as I've longed to do so with my writing.

---

[35] There's an intriguing story about Brubeck's faith journey here: http://bit.ly/2WOmya5 One reason I think he remains dear to my heart is that I was blessed to attend the world premiere of the Mass he composed – *To Hope: A Celebration* – at the National Shrine of Our Lady of the Snows in Belleville, IL in the 1980s.

And so, today, I pray:

God bless you, Dave! May the Lord grant you endless days to jam for all the hosts and dominions at the heavenly banquet. And thanks, from a deeply grateful heart, for your true companionship in these Forty Days!

– δδδ –

Scripture, to pray and ponder:

But [Namaan's] servants caught up with him and said, "Father, if the prophet had asked you to do something hard and heroic, wouldn't you have done it? So why not this simple 'wash and be clean'?" So he did it. He went down and immersed himself in the Jordan seven times, following the orders of the Holy Man. His skin was healed; it was like the skin of a little baby. He was as good as new.

2 Kings 5: 13-14

Day 21

Today's find: Altitude sickness

Apparently, I have entered some rarefied air in the WordPress blogosphere: When I posted my 20th entry yesterday, it touched off a bit of a digital party, courtesy of my gracious technology host.

The WordPress system generated an automated "congrats" message, viewable only on the *admin* page. I didn't get too excited over the accolade. I mean, geez, it came from a computer, right?

But truthfully, it did elicit a smile, as do the comments I receive from many who've been following along. And whether or not my readers comment, I feel blessed by *all* of you (as I said in my original invite to this space).

Then yesterday, something interesting happened: I got a couple of "likes" from people I don't know. I'm not exactly sure what that means – to have one's post "liked." But it actually felt kinda good. Through *Steadfast Spirit*, I'm now being blessed by perfect strangers!

On the other hand, I know from experience that attention-seeking can be a dangerous sensation. It's a great way to stunt both my writing and my spiritual growth. It plays out like ego intoxication: a kind of altitude sickness. It's as if I'm being led to the parapet of the temple. (Luke 4: 9-12) But instead of responding as Jesus does, I say to Satan, *"Tell me more…"*

So let me state, for the record, that this blog is *altogether gift*. I believe it has been given to me, and to the Giver belongs all the praise, the glory and the "likes." (Any errors, of course, are entirely my own.)

Let me also share a prayer with you today, which (when said meditatively) offers a sure-fire cure for altitude sickness, along with many other spiritual diseases. And why not? It comes, after all, from our mother, Mary:

> *My soul magnifies the Lord,*
> *My spirit rejoices in God my Savior.*
> *For he has looked with favor upon his lowly servant,*
> *From this day all generations shall call me blessed.*
> *The Almighty has done great things for me, and holy is his Name.*
>
> *He has mercy on those who fear him in every generation.*
> *He has shown strength of his arm:*
> *He has scattered the proud in their conceit.*
> *He has cast down the mighty from their thrones, and has lifted up the lowly.*
>
> *He has filled the hungry with good things;*
> *and the rich he has sent empty away.*
> *He has come to the help of his servant Israel, for he*

has remembered his promise of mercy, the promise he made to our fathers, to Abraham and his children forever. Amen.

P.S. Twenty posts: That means we're about half-way through Lent. *I'm just saying…*

– δδδ –

Scripture, to pray and ponder:

…with contrite heart and humble spirit let us be received; as though it were burnt offerings of rams and bullocks, or thousands of fat lambs, so let our sacrifice be in Your presence today as we follow You unreservedly; for those who trust in You cannot be put to shame. And now we follow You with our whole heart…

Daniel 3: 39-41

Day 22

Today's find: 'Not knowing'

It's been four days since Ellen and her companions left for their mission trip to Haiti,[36] and we haven't heard a peep.

That's actually good news. Due to the vagaries of the infrastructure there, we agreed before she set out that we wouldn't expect to hear from her unless something had gone wrong. So I'm happy, more or less, that our daughter has been *incommunicado* this week.

"Not knowing" can easily morph into something a bit more sinister, though, can't it? So often, we want to know, because "knowing" on some level gives us the impression of "control."

If I can just wrap my head around this challenge, then I can start *working* the problem. Defining the metrics. Picking the stage-gates. Reporting the progress.

"Knowing" is the first step in convincing myself that I can get this whole thing *fixed*, once and for all.

Except that's not really how things work, not all the time anyway.

---

[36] See 'Day 9', above

There are grievous hurts, there are diseases, there are sinful patterns, there are societal ills, there are disasters that I am utterly unable to control. And when I am confronted by them, the heart of the matter may well be figuring out how to find *grace*, rather than *anxiety*, in the "Not Knowing."

Can I let go of the need to be in control?

Can I trust that God's hand is at work, even when it's impossible to peer up around the bend?

I can't honestly say that's the sort of faith-walk I had in mind when I gave up on Game Six a couple of Octobers ago.[37] And, truthfully, it's been a bit of a struggle for me this week: my mind uneasy, even as my heart is confident that the Mighty One has good things in store for Ellen and the children she's met at *Ecole de L'enfant Jesus* in *Petit-Goâve*.

Which is to say, I am a work-in-progress when it comes to "Not Knowing." But every time I say "yes," every time I ask the Lord to bless my reluctance, God does in fact provide *"a lamp unto my feet."* (Psalm 119: 105) What's more, God's plans are always *bigger* than

---

[37] Yes, I gave up and went to bed before the end of the "David Freese Game" played by the St. Louis Cardinals in 2011 – missing out on one of the all-time classic conclusions to a World Series contest. My son later found something redeemable in my act of faithlessness: http://bit.ly/36DtafS

my plans, and potent enough to shine great light into some of the darkest places on earth.[38]

Given that bountiful history, what more, really, do I need to know?

– δδδ –

Scripture, to pray and ponder:

Just make sure you stay alert. Keep close watch over yourselves. Don't forget anything of what you've seen. Don't let your heart wander off. Stay vigilant as long as you live. Teach what you've seen and heard to your children and grandchildren.

Deuteronomy 4: 9

---

[38] And yet, I witnessed in April 2012 what was perhaps an even greater miracle than the Cardinals' comeback in Game Six: Christ's grace penetrating the walls of a supermax prison, and offering a spiritual freedom to men who were literally chained to the floor: http://bit.ly/1vm75c6

Day 23

Today's find: Precious blood

I cut myself shaving the other day, and – miracle of miracles – within a minute or two, the bleeding stopped and a tiny clot had formed.

Hyperbole, right?

A clot, *miraculous*? It's just a normal part of everyday life. In recent months, though, I've become a bit of a student regarding blood chemistry and the humble clot, discovering that there's a lot more there than meets the eye.

You see, the love of my life experienced a pulmonary embolism last July (a.k.a. "blood clot on the lungs"). And while spending time with Gerri in the hospital, I had a chance to read up on the clotting process.

The biochemist Michael Behe devotes an entire chapter (23 pages!) to the subject in his intriguing book, *Darwin's Black Box*.[39] He points out that the process is extremely complex, involving a delicately balanced and interconnected system of about 20 different proteins. Change any of those components,

---

[39] *Darwin's Black Box: The Biochemical Challenge to Evolution*, by Michael J. Behe. The Free Press.

even slightly, and the whole clotting system will fail. The clot won't form at the proper time, or in the proper place.

We've since learned that this is precisely what happened in Gerri's case. She has a "Protein-S" deficiency: one of those 20 pieces in the clotting cascade doesn't have all the parts it needs to function well. (We are blessed, by the way, to know that it's treatable. She's doing great since that initial episode.)

As for me, this recent shaving incident served as a timely Lenten reminder: Blood truly is something precious: both spectacularly complex and intricately designed to ensure that our tiny daily blunders don't turn into life-threatening disasters. (Note, too, that we haven't even talked about blood's role in nourishment, oxygenation or disease prevention. Our blood is a many splendored thing, indeed!)

So on this Lenten Friday, three weeks removed from Good Friday, I am moved to meditate on the One who designed our blood and its clotting action, in all its incredible interdependent detail.

How *wonderful* is this work!

How unfathomable, too, that the Brilliant Architect of blood clotting would willingly choose to let his own blood flow freely for me, for us, from the cross!

What do you want me to learn, dear Lord, in this gift you make to me of your Precious Blood?

— δδδ —

Scripture, to pray and ponder:

When they got to Jesus, they saw that he was already dead, so they didn't break his legs. One of the soldiers stabbed him in the side with his spear. Blood and water gushed out.

John 19: 33-34

Day 24

Today's find: Haitian hinges

It's been amazing to hear all the stories this week, as I have prayed (and asked others to pray) for Ellen and her companions during their mission trip to *Petit-Goâve*.[40]

Two out of three seem to have a Haiti connection themselves, either of a trip they've made, or someone close to them has made, to the impoverished nation. Invariably, they've been touched by unexpected encounters: gifts of "found spirituality" given by some of the poorest people on earth.

Just today, I heard another one. An ACTS teammate told me of the ingenious "Haitian hinge" he saw fashioned by a dad there, who was building a small toy-box for his son. The dad couldn't just head to a Lowes or a Home Depot; instead, he fabricated the hinge from two thin strips of copper.

He started by curling one edge on each strip; then, opposing those edges, he nested one curl inside the other, inserted a pin, and presto! A fully serviceable hinge, made from metal scraps – no coinage required!

---

[40] See 'Day 9', above.

My teammate had other stories, too. He recounted how another pair of Haitian acquaintances had worked to mend the zipper on a tent that *he* was ready to discard. We talked about the difference that encounter had revealed: the "opposing edges," if you will, between Americans, who tend to think of most things as disposable (and yet, we never seem to have enough) – and Haitians, who could find ingenious uses for materials that we'd consider scrap.

So who's teaching whom here? It got me thinking about a truth I have experienced on more than one occasion in recent years: Whenever we go to serve, even when we set out with the most altruistic of motives, we almost always find ourselves on the *receiving* end of abundant and unexpected graces. Our hearts expand, and we find ourselves *hinged* in unforgettable ways to other parts of the body of Christ.

I keep a free-verse poem framed in my office – a reflection that describes this mystery in a particularly captivating way. It was written by Mary Anne Grant, the daughter of dear friends, who died in Haiti some years ago when she travelled there on a mission trip as a high school senior. In my view, her words, and her life of loving service, leave no doubt that Mary Anne was connected to this great mystery.

I invite you now to consider them for yourself:

They live in the midst of poverty
Open wounds - Starvation
Crumbling houses
Trash in the streets
Debt - Failing crops
Contaminated water
Malnourished children
Disease
Desperation strikes.
Death seems inevitable.
So why do they smile?
Mary Anne Grant[41]

– 𝛿𝛿𝛿 –

Scripture, to pray and ponder:

One of the religion scholars came up. Hearing the lively exchanges of question and answer and seeing how sharp Jesus was in his answers, he put in his question: "Which is most important of all the commandments?" Jesus said, "The first in importance is, 'Listen, Israel: The Lord your God is one; so love the Lord God with all your passion and prayer and intelligence and energy.' And here is the second: 'Love others as well as you love yourself.' There is no other commandment that ranks with these."

Mark 12: 28-31

---

[41] Written by Mary Anne Grant in 1994 following a mission trip to Honduras as a junior in high school, and reprinted here with the permission of her parents, Bill and Anne Grant.

Day 25

Today's find: Cold Fact

I saw an astonishing movie last night: *Searching for Sugar Man*.[42] It's a documentary recounting the story of Rodriguez, the most famous rock star you've never heard of.

Rodriguez cut two albums in the early '70s – both of them, critically acclaimed and commercially disastrous in the United States. But half a world away, in South Africa, Rodriguez was *huge*: bigger than the Stones, bigger than the Beatles, according to the film.

As I'm watching the story unfold, I'm pretty sure I'm getting "Manti Téo-d" here.[43] How could it all possibly be true? A few minutes into the movie, I even Googled "Rodriguez" to see if I could determine whether he was/is real.

Improbable, yes. But it all checked out: Rodriguez's music may have crashed and burned in the States, but he was a very big deal indeed in South Africa – first, via pirated tapes, and later through re-released albums and CDs (*Cold Fact* and *Coming From Reality*) that sold

---

[42] Here's the movie's marketing website: http://bit.ly/32qG11B
[43] Remember Manti Téo? The Notre Dame football player who got elaborately hoaxed by a fake girlfriend? I didn't either until I clicked on this link: https://abcn.ws/2PZ1lJ4

hundreds of thousands of copies. The thing is, due to the economic boycott surrounding apartheid, Rodriguez neither knew about nor benefited from that localized fame.

There are lots of fascinating story lines in the film, but the one that struck me the most – and the one that turned into a tidbit of "found spirituality" – was how humble and peaceful the songwriter was when he was asked (some 30 years later) to reflect on the injustice of it all. "Wouldn't it have been nice to know that you could have been famous?" the filmmaker asks. And Rodriguez replies, "Well, I don't know how to respond to that. I don't know if it would have been for the better…"

There was something quite Christ-like in his willingness to deflect the desire for credit, the need to have his accomplishments recognized. It reminded me a bit of the reading we hear from Paul's second letter to the Corinthians (5: 17-21) at Mass:

> *…all this is from God, who has reconciled us to himself through Christ and given us the ministry of reconciliation, namely, God was reconciling the world to himself in Christ, not counting their trespasses against them and entrusting to us the message of reconciliation.*

Surely, Christ himself would have been a better ambassador for that message. But it's not how Jesus chose to accomplish this work in the world. Instead, Christ rolls the dice with us, in all our brokenness.

I've long been fascinated by Paul, and his particular role in spreading the Good News during the early years of the church. Brash, boisterous, self-confident: He was like the first rock-star of Christianity. And he certainly wasn't afraid of the spotlight: "Imitate me," he says in another letter. (2 Thessalonians 3: 7)

It's almost as if Christ chose to *use* Paul's enormous ego to give the Good News a little extra juice in those early days. Christ didn't mind disappearing a bit, personally, in order to let Paul's charisma and energy take center stage.

As for Paul: He certainly understood his brokenness, calling himself the least of the apostles – "one born abnormally." (1Cor 15:8) But he didn't let that stand in way of carrying out his mission for the Lord.

Neither, it seems, should we. Sure, each of us is sinful. That's a *Cold Fact*. But Christ says, "Do me a favor: Don't get hung up on that. I still love you. I have *always* loved you. And come on, let's go: We've got work to do!"

– δδδ –

Scripture, to pray and ponder:

Meanwhile the tax man, slumped in the shadows, his face in his hands, not daring to look up, said, "God, give mercy. Forgive me, a sinner."

Luke 18: 13

Day 26

Today's find: Hitting the wall

I did a double take at Mass yesterday, and it had nothing to do with the pink vestments.

Not directly anyway. But as our celebrant was explaining the reason for the shocking color of the chasuble, he said we were marking "the halfway point of Lent."[44] And I thought, "No way, José! We *gotta* be closer to the finish line than *that!*"

And in fact, we are: The real halfway point occurred sometime last week. It's just that we aren't all gathered as a community to mark the occasion, so Father was more or less taking good advantage of his larger audience on Sunday morning to make the point.

Of course, in some parts of our universal church, his opening statement would actually have been close to accurate. On Saturday, I learned that in the Syro-Malabar rite,[45] Lent is 50 days long. (I picked up that little tidbit while having lunch with our Associate Pastor, who grew up in that rite in his home state of Kerala, India.)

---

[44] Officially, "Laetare Sunday": http://bit.ly/2JZ3PmY
[45] Over 4 million Catholics in India consider this rite their home base: http://bit.ly/2K0oPJV

Don't know about you, but I've never really felt short-changed by a 40-day Lent. More often than not, I tend to hit the wall right about now. My resolutions have started to lose much of their appeal. My will weakens. My focus fades.

And as I was reflecting on the frailty of my spiritual condition, I was actually heartened by that notion of the 50-day Lent, going on halfway around the world from here. Or a bit more precisely, I was bolstered by the Body of Christ. It was a blessing to consider, for a moment, just how *big* our church is, how *diverse* it is, and how many hands there are to do the *heavy lifting* in the kingdom Jesus asks us to build.

That point was reinforced for me when I got a note from a dear friend the other day, who asked for prayers as she and her daughter head off to spend Spring Break on a mission trip to Belize. That's a cool thing, in and of itself. And making it even more cool is to know that they got connected to this trip through a Catholic high school in St. Louis, but they're teaming up with a Baptist church to do so. The Body of Christ, on mission together – many hands, making light work!

So I think I'm starting to catch my second wind here. And I have *you* – my sisters and brothers in Christ – to thank for it. *Your* faith and works make *mine* stronger.

– δδδ –

Scripture, to pray and ponder:

You groped your way through that murk once, but no longer. You're out in the open now. The bright light of Christ makes your way plain. So no more stumbling around. Get on with it! The good, the right, the true — these are the actions appropriate for daylight hours.

Ephesians 5: 8-9

Day 27

Today's find: Disordered affections

True Confessions time: I am not a big fan of the new translation of the Roman Missal.

This will come as absolutely no surprise to some of you, who've heard me rail and whine about the clunky sentence structures, the esoteric vocabulary, the unhelpful focus on merit and worthiness, etc. etc. etc. (I mean, really: When I say in the *confiteor* that "I have *greatly* sinned…", haven't I just committed *another* sin, the sin of pride? But I digress.)

On the other hand, I have begun to find a measure of grace in submitting to authority on this point. Even when the literally-translated words assault my ear, there's something to be said for being obedient in circumstances that I do not fully comprehend. And once in a while, that trickle of grace becomes a flood – as it did this morning, when our Pastor led us in the new Preface II of Lent[46] prior to the Eucharistic prayer.

He prayed, among other things, that we be "freed from disordered affections."

---

[46] You can find the entire text here: http://bit.ly/2ro31Sb

Ah, yes: disordered affections! What in the Sam Hill[47] are *they?*

Then I realized: This clunky term had stopped me in my tracks, long enough to consider what they meant, and whether in fact disordered affections might be a part of my life.

Upon further review, I had to admit that they are: My "favorite" sins. My disordered desire to *cling* to my brokenness, rather than embrace the saving power of the cross.

In today's Gospel reading (John 5: 1-16), I met a man like me: the one who had been waiting for 38 years in the portico of the Temple, hoping for the waters to stir in the pool called Bethesda.

Jesus asks him, "Do you want to be well?" Interestingly, he doesn't give Jesus a direct answer. For some reason, in that moment, he seems to find more comfort in his long habit of brokenness than in the saving grace that Jesus is offering him.

A disordered affection, indeed.

—

[47] Did you know that 'Sam Hill' is a euphemism for 'the devil'? http://bit.ly/2rg1Dkn

Save me, Lord Jesus, from myself…and from my cherished habits of sinfulness. Help me to say "Yes!" to the ever-present offer of your grace!

– δδδ –

Scripture, to pray and ponder:

[God says]: "Pay close attention now: I'm creating new heavens and a new earth. All the earlier troubles, chaos, and pain are things of the past, to be forgotten.

Isaiah 65: 17

Day 28

Today's find: Tom Petty, Prophet

The Holy Spirit has been quiet today. Too quiet.

Since the beginning of Lent, I've noticed that each day's topic of "found spirituality" has turned up pretty early on – usually in the pre-dawn hours, and never later than the beginning of my work day.

The pattern was broken today, though. Lunchtime came, and a slight feeling of panic set in. *"I got NOTHIN'!"* I realized, as my ego (all too easily bruised by perceived failures) started setting off a few alarms.

Didn't like the sensation, of course. It felt a little like abandonment: *"C'mon, God: gimme what I need! And here, by the way, is the schedule that would be most convenient for me."* As I was turning up the volume on that refrain, all of a sudden, another familiar lyric popped into my consciousness.

If you listened to rock in the '70s and '80s, you probably know where I'm going with this: Tom Petty the Heartbreaker, today had become for me Tom

Petty the Prophet, reminding me that the *waiting* is often the hardest part.[48]

Given the way my musical memory works, it was just a short jump from there to recognize that Petty could be counted on for more than one spiritual insight. Feeling lost and alone, abandoned by God? Well, I suppose you don't really have to live like a *refugee*. (Ahem.)

At which point, the Holy Spirit gave me a dope slap, and said, "John, we were just talking about the virtue of patience here. Can we refocus a bit?"

I had a sneaking suspicion about where my memory was about to be led *next:* to one of my favorite reflections, penned by one of my favorite spiritual writers, Pierre Teilhard de Chardin, SJ. It's called *Patient Trust.*[49] Its "money line" goes like this:

> *Only God could say what this new spirit*
> *gradually forming within you will be.*
> *Give Our Lord the benefit of believing*
> *that his hand is leading you,*
> *and accept the anxiety of feeling yourself*
> *in suspense and incomplete.*

---

[48] Petty's music video of *The Waiting* can be found here: https://youtu.be/uMyCa35_mOg ; and his video for *Refugee* here: https://youtu.be/fFnOfpIJL0M

[49] Read the text of the entire prayer here: http://bit.ly/2NQJ7qE

Wonderful words to *contemplate*. And (as I have discovered yet again today) words that are very difficult to *live*. Waiting often *is* the hardest part.

– δδδ –

Scripture, to pray and ponder:

God is a safe place to hide, ready to help when we need him. We stand fearless at the cliff-edge of doom, courageous in seastorm and earthquake, before the rush and roar of oceans, the tremors that shift mountains. Jacob-wrestling God fights for us, God of angel armies protects us.

Psalm 46: 1-3

Day 29

Today's find: A tilted globe

Well, "my guy" didn't get the nod yesterday.[50] Still, I am delighted at the prospect of a Pope named Francis.

Not that anyone asked, but I was pulling for the Franciscan – Cardinal Sean O'Malley – to be elected to the chair of St. Peter.

Admittedly, I am a "homer," and therefore, it's only natural that I'd put an American at the top of my list. (As for Cardinal Timothy Dolan: He hails from Holy Infant Parish in Ballwin[51] – arch-rivals, at least on the soccer field, to my own parish, St. Joe's of Manchester – so there's *no way* I could root for a "Holy Infant" guy.) (Just kidding. I think.)

Truth is, I don't know a lot about Cardinal O'Malley, but I am drawn to his Franciscan spirituality and how he has apparently applied those graces to his work in Boston. It seems, at least from the outside, like a discipline that might be useful in addressing some of the recent conflicts within the Curia. So if it's not to

---

[50] Argentina's Cardinal Jorge Bergoglio was elected pope on March 13, 2013, taking the name Francis.
[51] Both are actually fine Missouri parishes, despite their rivalry in sports: http://bit.ly/2oYsyjW and http://bit.ly/2K3u8Zd

be the Franciscan who will shepherd the Church, then a Pope named Francis is probably the next best thing.

The fact that Pope Francis comes to us from "the ends of the earth" is likely to be a blessing, too, I think.[52] That notion was crystallized for me yesterday, as I listened to the daily meditation offered online by the Jesuits of Great Britain.[53] One passage in particular caught my ear:

> *Originally the word 'Lent' comes to us from an Old English word, simply meaning 'spring.' Perhaps we would do well to think of Lent as the greening time of year, in the northern hemisphere at least.*

Indeed, I have long found spiritual encouragement in this very link between Lent and spring. Until yesterday, though, it had never occurred to me that *half* the world's people (and a significant majority of the earth's Catholics[54]) don't have the benefit of such a connection between spiritual and seasonal renewal. As they pray their way through Lent, the leaves are falling off the trees.

---

[52] Remember how the selection of this pope from Argentina caught us all a little off-guard? https://on.wsj.com/33uHipJ
[53] Pray-As-You-Go is a wonderful resource for daily meditations: http://bit.ly/2JXkzuT
[54] Turns out, our global Catholic faith family is heavily weighted toward the southern hemisphere: http://bit.ly/33v6Nr6

Presumably, a Pope born in Argentina can help open our "northern" eyes to this reality – and perhaps challenge some of our other cherished assumptions, too. It should be exciting to see what spiritual gifts this papacy will bring to the church.

Today, though, it's enough simply to note the wry smile on my lips as I consider the globe that sits in my office. It's tilted on its axis, you see – so that, no matter how you spin it, the countries of the northern hemisphere always turn up at eye level.

Might the Holy Spirit, through the elevation of a Latin American pope, be inviting me to tilt this world (not to mention, many elements of the *real* world) in some other, more fruitful directions?

– δδδ –

Scripture, to pray and ponder:

I didn't keep the news of Your ways a secret, didn't keep it to myself. I told it all, how dependable You are, how thorough. I didn't hold back pieces of love and truth for myself alone. I told it all, let the congregation know the whole story.

Psalm 40: 10

Day 30

Today's find: Futile gestures

There's not a doubt in my mind that Jesus was courageous – even the most courageous person who ever lived. It took guts for him to open his arms on the cross, especially since few, if any, of the "real men" in his company saw much point in this act of sacrifice.

Jesus was courageous, yes. But not foolhardy. You learn that about Jesus when you consider the opening lines from the Gospel passage (John 7: 1) we heard at Mass:

> *Jesus moved about within Galilee; he did not wish to travel in Judea, because the Jews were trying to kill him.*

Jesus *did* eventually head south to Judea, of course – entering Jerusalem and walking right into the arms of those who meant him harm. But for a time at least, the Galilean ministry seems to have been enough. It was a fruitful place for Jesus to scatter the seeds of the Good News.

I was intrigued by that little insight into Jesus' daily movements, because it reminded me of the story I'd read early in Lent about the Martyrs of the White Rose.

Imagine living in Munich, during the height of Nazi power – knowing that much of what the government was doing was wrong; knowing, too, that your political leaders did not welcome opposing views. What the heck are you supposed to do?

Hans and Sophie Scholl (a brother and sister, in their early 20s) decided it was time to speak the truth to power. They organized a group of university students called The White Rose, and started fanning out through the city to circulate a series of leaflets.

The tracts exposed the abuses of the Nazi regime, urging citizens to revolt. On February 18, 1943, Hans and Sophie were caught distributing the sixth leaflet, and after four days of intense interrogation (during which they refused to identify the other members of the group), they were beheaded for treason.

What a blessing it was for me to read about their leafleting, their courage. I suspect the Scholls knew that this home-brewed apostolate of theirs might not end well. I imagine they understood, too, that they were probably tilting at windmills. What good could amateur leaflets, distributed in one little corner of the Third Reich, possibly do?

If you think about it though, the Scholls were actually following Jesus' example. They had embraced his model of the seemingly futile gesture. They trusted that God's grace would be enough to transform the work of their hands, and multiply its effect, in ways they might never live to see.

But does that mean we are called to spend our entire lives or invest all our energies in such activities? Probably not, if you check out Jesus' lead: There's a time when we are called to "move about Galilee," just as there may be a time when we are called "to the cross."

> *Lord, grant me the serenity to accept the things I cannot change; courage to change the things I can; and wisdom to know the difference.*[55]

– δδδ –

Scripture, to pray and ponder:

[Jesus said] "I am not interested in crowd approval."

John 5: 41

---

[55] Here's a little history about one of the modern world's most famous prayers: http://bit.ly/2Q0H7yO

Day 31

Today's find: Parishioner – what's in a word?

I spent the morning at our beautiful new Parish Center attending the bi-annual Pastoral Assembly. About 50 others (from our total congregation of about 9,000) were there, too – all, familiar faces and many of them, very dear friends. What a blessing to be there, surrounded by so many joyful active members of our community! A reminder in flesh and blood that the Body of Christ is living and effective in Manchester.

Not that we're a perfect parish. Far from it. In fact, the primary order of business was to review progress on several key improvement initiatives now under way.

But to me, the thing that set the tone for a particularly uplifting session was the comment our pastor made at the outset. "Do we have enough *volunteers* at St. Joe's?" he asked. "That's really the wrong question. You are *parishioners*. Or as I prefer to pronounce it, *parish-owners*. By your involvement, you demonstrate the conviction that you have an ownership stake here."

I took a moment to let that concept settle in: Parish-owners.

How radically it changes the calculation! I'm an *owner* – not merely a customer of, or a participant in, all that my parish has to offer.

I'm an owner: So if the liturgies are dull, at least part of that is on me.

I'm an owner: So if there are needs that aren't being met in the community, then look in the mirror to assess a share of the responsibility.

I'm an owner: So when the Good News starts to take root and grow somewhere around St. Joe's, it's OK to let my heart be warmed, and to share in the praise: "well done, my good and faithful servant." (Matthew 25: 21)

How different that notion of ownership seems, compared to the attitude Jesus encounters in the members of "the crowd" in today's Gospel reading. (John 7: 40-53) Presumably, these people were all part of a faith community, too. But their voices take on an entirely different tone. They tend to nitpick: "The Christ can't come from Galilee, can he?" They are quick to mock: "Have you also been deceived?" And accuse: "Are you one of those Galileans, too?"

Interestingly, the episode ends not in communion, but with *separation*. "Then each went to his own house," the evangelist says.

So now, I'm beginning to wonder: Might ownership in my community be a far more important aspect of faith life than I ever imagined?

Or put another way: Is it possible to be "a person of God" without *also* being part of "a people of God"?

— δδδ —

Scripture, to pray and ponder:

If your heart is broken, you'll find God right there; if you're kicked in the gut, [God will] help you catch your breath. Disciples so often get into trouble; still, God is there every time.

Psalm 34: 18-19

Day 32

Today's find: Parishioners, wayfarers

Among the topics discussed at the Pastoral Assembly was St. Joe's upcoming 150th anniversary celebration. So take a moment to let *that* idea soak into your bones: All the holy people, the generous people, who have been encountering the Lord through this community in Manchester since the time of the Civil War.

If we are a vibrant, caring, witnessing, educating, loving community today, it's due in part to the work and faith of the many, many generations who have come before us on this holy hill in suburban St. Louis.

There's a depth and solidity to our parish that can be of great comfort, at times. When we go through struggles, when we consider our challenges, it can bolster our spirits to know that St. Joe's has probably been through something quite similar before.

But that's not the same thing as saying we're a "faith" community, is it? The beginning of our parish mission statement captures that idea a bit more precisely: We declare that we are a "Christ-centered family…"

Christ is the source of our faith – not our long history, or our wonderful facilities, or our extraordinary pastoral staff, or our incredible people.

Christ is at the heart of who we are.

And *in* that reality, we are like every parish that has ever been formed. I gained an insight into what that means earlier this year, while reading a collection entitled *Early Christian Writings* (a Christmas present from one of my sons.) The volume contains letters from Clement, Polycarp, Barnabas and others.

The writings are pretty cool, in and of themselves. But it was a footnote to one of the letters that really caught my eye. In translating the Greek salutation to the Christian community (*paroikos*), the editor said in effect that the closest term we have in English is "transients" or "resident aliens." And, he notes, "It became a favorite description of the Christian community in any locality, and has eventually made its way into the English language as 'parish'."

How startling to realize that, on some fundamental level, when we call ourselves "parish," we are calling ourselves "migrants." We are, at our core, a pilgrim people. Strangers in a strange land. Our *true* identity is in Christ.

Some years ago, author and poet Kathleen Norris[56] introduced me to a passage from St. Augustine that

---

[56] You can find summaries of Norris' earliest books here: http://bit.ly/32qxI5X

has helped me grow to appreciate this concept much more deeply. It goes like this:

> *"Let us sing alleluia here on earth, while we still live in anxiety, so that we may sing it one day in heaven…in full security. God's praises are sung both here and there. Here they are sung by those destined to die…there, by those destined to live forever. Here, they are sung in hope…there, in hope's fulfillment. Here, they are sung by pilgrims; there, they are sung by people living in their own country. So let us sing now, not in order to enjoy a life of leisure, but in order to lighten our labors. We should sing as pilgrims do. We should sing, but continue our journey. Sing then, but keep going."*

So it seems that "parish-owners" doesn't capture the full meaning of "parishioners," all by itself. We are owners, yes. But it might be beneficial to consider how we are called to be wayfarers, too.

– δδδ –

Scripture, to pray and ponder:

[God], publish Your mandate for us. You get us ready for life: You probe for our soft spots, You knock off our rough edges.

Psalm 7: 9

Day 33

Today's find: Bracketology

For some, it's St. Patrick's Day that fosters temptation. For others (like me), it's college basketball – an admittedly disordered affection, plopped right down in the middle of Lent – that entices me off the beam of my best intentions for this holy season.

Today, of course, is Bracket Monday: a dark, spinning vortex of seduction for any fan of the sport, inviting us to sink hours of otherwise potentially productive time into a mere amusement, picking "our teams" for the Big Dance that begins on Thursday.

Perhaps this is a rationalization, but as I take note of my itchy trigger finger (just dying to start penciling in the first draft of my Big Dance Bracket) it occurs to me that there may be some "found spirituality" in the art and science of Bracketology.

So work with me here: There are basically two schools of Bracketology, two methods for picking a winning assortment of teams in a tournament legendary for its upsets.

The first method relies on Blind Luck/Faith. You pick your teams randomly, or based on your affection for the school mascot, or because your third cousin

Herbert has a son who played in the marching band there some years ago.

The second method relies on Informed Opinion. You've done a little homework, so you know the strengths and tendencies (and weaknesses) of at least some of the teams. And you check out Expert Opinions to help make your bracket picks for the rest.

Frankly, either method is just as likely to produce a winner. But no self-respecting college b-ball fan would ever admit that the Blind Luck method is an acceptable way to collect the winnings from the office pool.

Here's the thing, though: You can wind up being just as blind as the other guy when you rely on Method Two, and give the Experts power over your picks. After all, how much do you really know about their expertise? How reliable is their analysis? How much bias or prejudice might there be in their world-views?

Jesus, it turns out, chides the Pharisees in the gospel reading of the day (John 8: 12-20) for relying too much on the testimony of Experts when it comes to matters of the kingdom. "You do not know where I came from, and where I am going," he reminds them. "If you knew me, you would know my Father, also."

It's as if he's inviting them – inviting *us* – to take the plunge. To get to know him, personally, before we decide to cast our lot with him. The Experts can be helpful, he seems to say. But there's nothing like a personal encounter to help you appreciate Jesus as the light of the world. And from there, when you choose to follow him, you have his promise that "you will not walk in darkness."

—

P.S. Here's a 'Bracket Tip' from a SLU Billiken Expert: Take them at least into the Sweet Sixteen…and even Elite Eight, if you dare![57]

– 𝛿𝛿𝛿 –

Scripture, to pray and ponder:

Martha said, "[Jesus], if you'd been here, my brother wouldn't have died. Even now, I know that whatever you ask God, [God] will give you."

John 11: 21-22

---

[57] Of course, my Bracketology advice was deeply flawed and hopelessly optimistic. But here's proof that I wasn't alone on the Billiken bandwagon in 2013: http://bit.ly/2WTYWRg

Day 34

Today's find: The Joe we know

Did you ever notice how St. Joseph was always on the go? Nazareth to Bethlehem. Bethlehem to Egypt. Egypt to Nazareth. Nazareth to Jerusalem, and back again. (Matthew 2: 1, 14, 19-20, 22-23)

That's actually one of the very few things we know about this saintly Joe, whose feast day we celebrate on March 19.

We also learn in scripture that he was a "righteous" man, one whose sense of justice was infused with incredible compassion. What a contrast, to compare *his* reaction to the news that Mary had been found pregnant, to the clamor of the scribes and Pharisees against the woman "caught in adultery." (John 8: 3-11)

This is a Joe I think we'd all like to know. An ordinary Joe, whose extraordinary faith is perhaps obscured by the honors and titles we have conferred upon him over the centuries: "Saint Joseph, Provider and Protector of the Holy Family"; "Saint Joseph, Patron of the Universal Church."

Indisputably, Joseph had an important role to play in salvation history. And no doubt, he received ample graces to help him faithfully discharge that role.

But it's also pretty clear (from the few nuggets available to us in scripture) that Joseph didn't have the benefit of a heavenly GPS as he journeyed in faith with Mary, and then Jesus. He didn't have a lot of detail to go on. No master plan guiding his movements. No career path fully outlined and charted. Indeed, even the plans he *did* make initially – to take a bride and start a family – wound up undergoing some pretty significant rewrites.

And yet, that never seemed to keep Joseph from taking the next step forward. Peter Mayer sings a beautiful song in tribute to the saint's indomitable spirit, called *Hey Joseph*.[58]

I think Peter Mayer has it right: What a gift this ordinary Joe gives us, by his determination to keep walking even when the reasons or the outcome are not in the least bit clear.

– δδδ –

Scripture, to pray and ponder:

I'll never quit telling the story of Your love – how You built the cosmos and guaranteed everything in it. Your love has always been our lives' foundation, Your fidelity has been the roof over our world.

Psalm 89: 2-3

---

[58] Here's the music video: https://youtu.be/9v5gkE-dpoE

Day 35

Today's find: Praise

I spent a little time with the prophet Daniel this morning. And frankly, he started to get on my nerves just a tad.

Actually, I'm fascinated by all the stories found in the book of Daniel. I was intrigued, too, to discover some years ago the litanies of praise that are recorded there.

The first time I heard excerpts from one of the litanies, I thought I must be listening to a Psalm. But no: There it is, plunked down in the middle of Chapter 3 – Shadrach, Meshach and Abednego, bursting forth in song as they milled about in Nebuchadnezzar's fiery furnace.

And sing the three brothers did. And sing. And sing. And sing. For a total of 38 verses. (Daniel 3: 52-90)

About halfway through, I'm going, "OK! Enough already! I get the point: God is worthy to be praised, in all God's works!" (Let's just hope God wasn't listening to *that* petulant little outburst on my part!)

If there is a blessing to be found in my impatience, though, perhaps it's this: My encounter with the litany got me wondering why we praise God in the first place. God certainly doesn't need our affirmation.

Our words add nothing to God's works. So what, precisely, is the point of praise?

There's some wisdom regarding that very question in the Catechism of the Catholic Church.[59] It tells us that adoration and praise are "the first attitude of man, acknowledging that he is a creature before his Creator." (CCC: 2628)

Creature, yes. And one whose heart has been touched by Creator.

God has put *joy* in my heart. I know it's there, even though I'm not always attuned to its Presence. When I *do* feel the joy, though, I realize that it is often expressed in praise. How can I keep from singing?

And here's the remarkable thing: I live in the age of the Hubble Telescope. Aided by technology, I have been able to peer much more deeply into the cosmos than Shadrach, Meshach and Abednego ever could.

I know, indisputably, that my presence here and now is but an infinitesimal speck of cosmic dust.

And yet, I am not overlooked by the Creator.

God chooses to send signals – to send joy – into my heart. God chooses to know me, to know *us*. God

---

[59] The entire Catechism is available online, here: http://bit.ly/2NWGBio

chooses to build a loving relationship with us. Imagine *that!*

—

God of Wonder – You are worthy to be praised! Always, and everywhere…praised!

– δδδ –

Scripture, to pray and ponder:

Blessed are You, O Lord, the God of our fathers, praiseworthy and exalted above all forever…

Daniel 3: 52

Day 36

Today's find: Whippersnappers

Jesus is mixing it up with the elders again in the Gospel reading of the day. (John 8: 51-59) And their first take is that he's got a screw loose. *"Now, we are sure that you are possessed,"* they say.

Soon enough, though, the conversation takes a different turn as the Old Guard sets its defenses firmly in place: *"Who do you make yourself out to be?"*

And at last, they play the trump card: *"You are not yet 50 years old…"*

A bracing comment – at least, for someone like me who happens to have passed that chronological marker some years ago.

Because I've been around the block a few times, I am inclined on occasion to think that I have seen it all. Had I been in the crowd around Jesus that day, I'm not sure how I would have taken what I heard from that young whippersnapper. (Or the wisdom I hear from any young whippersnapper, for that matter!)

But what do I *miss* when I rely too much on my own experience, or on the collective wisdom of the crowd around me?

In Sirach (24: 26-27), we read:

> *The first human being never finished comprehending wisdom, nor will the last succeed in fathoming her. For deeper than the sea are her thoughts, and her counsels deeper than the great abyss.*

Wisdom, indeed, has provided for us a Savior. But this Savior is not at all like the great leader or powerful warrior that we would expect.

Instead, the Christ comes to us a defenseless child. He grows "in wisdom and age and favor before God and man" (Luke 2: 52) until the point, of course, when he starts saying things that we find difficult to believe. Things that don't quite sync up with our experience. And then, he surprises us *again* by opening his arms on the cross.

This is strange wisdom, isn't it?

Certainly stranger than the looniest idea I've heard from any other young whippersnapper in my 50+ years on earth. It's impossible to wrap my mind around.

And perhaps that's precisely point. Jesus is looking to move not just my mind, but also my heart. He's inviting me to always keep myself open to new possibilities, in and through *him*.

– δδδ –

Scripture, to pray and ponder:

They spoke out against God and Moses: "Why did you drag us out of Egypt to die in this godforsaken country? No decent food; no water – we can't stomach this stuff any longer."

Numbers 21: 5

Day 37

Today's find: My rock. My cave.

One of the great recent blessings in my life was the chance to spend a little time in the desert southwest. We call it our "Grand Canyon" vacation. But in truth, a side trip to Monument Valley[60] in southern Utah was my favorite stop along the way.

The scenery there is spectacular. And by luck of the draw (or God-incidence, perhaps?), our little traveling party wound up with a private tour – just the four of us in an open Jeep, with Leroy our Navajo guide.

Leroy didn't want to be there that day. He'd been called in to help handle the overflow of tourists on a sunny Saturday afternoon. But something about entering into this sacred desert space changed his mood. Before long, he was taking us to places that not everyone gets to see. And he was telling us stories that not every tourist is patient enough to hear.

He showed us one spot in particular that captured my fancy: An enormous slab of sandstone perched at an angle against an even more enormous butte. "When we see a leaning rock like this," he said, "it tells us the Spirit is within." Then he went on to recount the story

---

[60] More about Monument Valley can be found here: http://bit.ly/2WVRcyc

of a shaman who had shown up at the tribal park headquarters one day, asking to be taken to *this* spot.

The pilgrim had traveled from somewhere in Europe, and though it was his first visit to America, he seemed to know all about this particular leaning rock. And he needed to be there, to circle around behind the slab, slip into the coolness and quiet of the small cave whose entrance it protected, and simply experience spiritual *energy* he found there.

With Leroy's permission, I too spent some time in the shaman's cave and found comfort there. I was in the middle of the desert, but for a moment, I felt completely protected and secure. Later in the day, I journaled about the experience – reflecting about Elijah and his experience on a similar kind of holy ground. (1 Kings 19: 12-13)

All those memories came rushing back to me this morning, when I joined in reciting the responsorial psalm (Psalm 18: 2-3) at Mass.

> *I love you, O Lord, my strength,*
> *O Lord, my rock, my fortress, my deliverer.*

I remembered experiencing the comfort of the cave, behind the rock. I remembered, too, how terribly *exposed* the rocks themselves were, throughout Monument Valley. If you're clinging to a rock there, you're probably feeling anything *but* comfort. In fact, your life is probably in danger.

And I found an unexpected blessing in that contrast between rock and cave. The Lord, it seems, promises to be with us in *both* situations.

The Lord is near when we enter into the stillness and quiet. The Lord is *also* near when we feel horribly exposed.

And I could understand, at last, the words spoken by Jeremiah (20: 13) when all his world seemed to be crashing in upon him:

> *Sing to the Lord! Praise the Lord!*
> *For he has rescued the life of the poor from the power*
> *of the wicked!*

What a blessing, to be able to sing in *every* circumstance of life, because we know the Lord, our Rock, is near!

– δδδ –

Scripture, to pray and ponder:

So if the Son sets you free, you are free through and through.

John 8: 36

Day 38

Today's find: Scapegoat or Lamb?

With Palm Sunday close at hand, we focused quite a bit on Jesus' passion and death during our ACTS team meeting. And I heard it again, the phrase that always seems to roil my spirit just a bit: *"Jesus died for our sins."*

It's a disturbing notion to me, particularly when it's portrayed in a *transactional* sense: A blood-thirsty God demanding reparations for our offenses. Frankly, if that's what it means to be saved, then I'm not sure I want any part of it. It's really nothing more than a recipe for *revenge*, the lowest form of relationship.

Not that this is an obscure or esoteric way to interpret the phrase. I'd wager that at least half of all Christians have something like a scapegoat in mind when they consider the concept: They're lining up behind the High Priest of the Israelites as he lays all the sins, faults and transgressions of the people on the goat's head before it is driven out into the desert to die. (Leviticus 16: 15)

The Franciscan Richard Rohr[61] has a good way of expressing my dis-ease with the whole concept of sacrificial atonement. It *"makes God appear rather petty*

---

[61] Some people find Rohr's concepts challenging, but on the whole, I think his spirituality is refreshing and insightful: http://bit.ly/2CpCF4t

and powerless" he says. *"Is God that unfree to love and forgive?"*

But if God *isn't* demanding tit-for-tat, a princely ransom for our sins, then why precisely *did* Jesus have to die?

For me, a better image is not the scapegoat, but the Lamb. It's a title for Christ that appears again and again in Revelation, and I believe it provides an important insight into what gives Jesus his power when he's lifted high upon the cross.

Jesus saves, it seems, because he is willing to *empty* himself, to lay his life down like a lamb. He does not cling to his birthright. He does not demand to have what he rightfully *deserves* as the Son of God. Which, if you think about it, is the exact *opposite* of human wisdom.

Humans believe we can find happiness in the things we buy or in the power we possess. Jesus saves us from ourselves, by showing us a different way. A better way. He *empties* himself of every possession, even his basic dignity. And what does he find there, in the emptiness?

Jesus discovers that he is *still* God's beloved one. In fact, in the glory of the resurrection, it seems like Jesus has drawn even closer to his heavenly Father than when he started out. (See Philippians 2: 5-11)

And here's the Good News: Jesus tells us that the same path is open to *us*, as well. We are God's beloved, not because of what we own, or what we accomplish, or even because of what we repent of in our lives.

We are God's beloved simply because that is what the Holy One created us to be.

The wisdom of Jesus, then – and the message of the cross – is that salvation cannot be earned. It is God's *gift* to us through the death and resurrection of the self-sacrificing Jesus. And that truly is Good News, because when we finally accept the gift, that's when we realize that there is nothing, absolutely nothing, about which we need to be afraid.

– δδδ –

Scripture, to pray and ponder:

[Jesus said], "I say this with absolute confidence. If you practice what I'm telling you, you'll never have to look death in the face."

John 8: 51

Day 39

Today's find: Hosanna, Ducks.

I suppose I should tip my cap to the Oregon Ducks, but my heart's not in it.

You see, the Ducks put a whuppin' on my beloved Saint Louis University Billikens last night, denying SLU its first-ever trip to the Sweet Sixteen of the NCAA basketball tourney.[62]

After watching the Bills crash and burn, I think I'm developing a deeper appreciation for why they call it "March Madness." I was mad as H-E-double-toothpicks as I watched the game unfold. Gone was the extraordinary cohesiveness and heads-up play I witnessed a week ago, as the Billikens were putting the finishing touches on their double championship in the A-10 conference.[63]

My boys looked like world-beaters then: Able to take a worthy opponent's best shot, and still come out on top. Last night, in contrast, SLU crumpled like a cheap suit.

---

[62] Some say there was a moral victory to be found in the beat-down. But I'm really not into moral victories on the hardwood. http://bit.ly/2Cpz5XU

[63] The Billikens' best was simply not good enough this year: http://bit.ly/2pXLfVk

So yeah: Hosanna, Ducks. Yippee ki-yay.

And my, how *quickly* things can change.

Honestly, I wish I didn't have to blog on Palm Sunday about the brutal finish to SLU's season. I don't need the reminder about how empty "Hosannas" can be.

Or perhaps I do.

Perhaps this is the perfect time for me to contemplate the model that Jesus gives us at the beginning of Holy Week.

It's interesting, isn't it, that the Master is an active participant in the scenario that leads up to his triumphant entrance into Jerusalem. Jesus sends two disciples to fetch him a colt. He makes a conscious choice to mount up, an action that prompts the accolades of the crowd. (Luke 19: 30-40) And just as consciously, Jesus embraces the journey to the cross as the week progresses.

It's almost as if Jesus wants to make sure that we see the contrast here. He wants to make sure that we are prepared for what lies ahead, *all* of it. Sure, there will be joys and successes. Maybe lots of them. But tough times are part of the deal, too. And so we need to keep our eyes on the prize.

Author Father Ronald Rolheiser, OMI puts it this way[64]:

> ...what we need when we are in a 'dark night' isn't the well-intentioned sympathy of a friend who wants to rescue us from the pain, but the wisdom of the mystics who tell us: When you lose your securities, when you find yourself in an emotional and spiritual free-fall, when you are in the belly of the whale, let go, detach yourself, let the pain carry you to where it needs to take you, don't resist; rather weep, wail, cry, and put your mouth to the dust, and wait.
>
> Just wait.
>
> You are like a baby being weaned from its mother's breast and forced to learn a new way of nourishing yourself. Anything you do to stop what's happening will only delay the inevitable, the pain that must be gone through in order come to a new maturity.

So enjoy the ride, Ducks. But take it from a chastened Billken fan: It's probably best if you don't get too comfortable.

---

[64] Used with permission of the author, Oblate Father Ron Rolheiser. Currently, Father Rolheiser is serving as President of the Oblate School of Theology in San Antonio Texas. He can be contacted through his website, www.ronrolheiser.com. Follow on Facebook www.facebook.com/ronrolheiser.

– 𝛿𝛿𝛿 –

Scripture, to pray and ponder:

I followed orders, stood there and took it while they beat me, held steady while they pulled out my beard, didn't dodge their insults, faced them as they spit in my face.

Isaiah 50: 6

Day 40

Today's find: Taking my rubbish to the curb.

It was a gorgeous day in the St. Louis area Saturday – had that "first day of spring" kind of feel to it. Bright sunshine, balmy temperatures. The *perfect* day to do that deep pruning on the landscaping out front.

By the time I was done, I was surprised at how much yard waste the project generated. I knew the bushes were overgrown, but 12 bags' worth of branches, thorns and stems? It made for an impressive pile at the curb (and I whispered a prayer of gratitude for the guy who would haul it all away for us this week.)

Now, if you've been following along, you may recall that I attached a certain amount of Lenten symbolism to this particular home-improvement project. *What things, like my overgrown yews, are preventing other, more fruitful things from entering into my life?*[65]

And: *Let's make this holy season a time when I seek the grace to take care of them, once and for all.*

In a very real sense, then, Saturday's beautiful weather was a gift from God to me. I hope the rest of you enjoyed it, too. But it was truly special for me – a

---

[65] See 'Day 19', above.

chance to get the bushes trimmed, before Easter, and to consider the other ways that God has been working in my life throughout these 40 days.

There have been ups and downs, to be sure. Joys[66] and heartaches.[67] Surprises, too: Extraordinary little gifts from the Holy One that no one in the world (except perhaps for my dear wife Gerri) might fully appreciate.

And then came Sunday.

Less than 17 hours after I hauled the last bag of my yard waste to the curb, it began to snow.

This is March 24th, mind you: Half-a-week into spring in the northern hemisphere[68] and a week away from Easter. Still, there was snow. And not just a few timid flakes, but a veritable blizzard. Nearly a foot of snow by the time the storm had passed.

So when I looked out the window this morning, God had yet another surprise in store for me: My Lenten rubbish, still stacked at the curb, but now covered in a luxuriously deep, pure, white blanket.

All the world is covered, too, I suppose – or at least, our little corner of it.

---

[66] See 'Day 7', above...
[67] ...And 'Day 39'...
[68] ...And 'Day 29'.

Still, it took my breath away, to consider what a great gift the Lord had in store for me this Lent. What a great gift God offers to *all* of us – the chance to take our rubbish to the curb, and then have it transformed into something beautiful. Something we never would have expected. Something that at first glance might seem impossible.

While I'm not exactly sure how to respond to God's gift, Psalm 57 seems like a good place to start:

> *My heart is ready, O God*
> *My heart is ready.*
> *I will sing, I will sing your praise.*
> *Awake, my soul!*
> *Awake, lyre and harp!*
> *I will awake the dawn!*

– δδδ –

Scripture, to pray and ponder:

"Take a good look at my servant. I'm backing him to the hilt. He's the one I chose, and I couldn't be more pleased with him. I've bathed him with my Spirit, my life."

Isaiah 42: 1

Day 41

Today's find: Giving it away

Some of the holiest people I know are those who have encountered Christ through the 12 Steps. (Or more accurately, those who have encountered a Power greater than themselves in and through their programs.)

Among the *other* holiest people I know on earth are those I have met "inside the joint" through Kairos Prison Ministry in recent years.

Both groups are on my mind and in my heart today.

I'm thinking about the 12-Steppers because of the wisdom they have shown me, particularly in the 12th Step itself: *"Having had a spiritual awakening as a result of these Steps, we tried to carry this message to others, and to practice these principles in all our affairs."*

In other words, you haven't *really* had a spiritual awakening unless and until you pass it on. Until you give it away.

It's the kind of philosophy that might even take you to prison, if that's where the Spirit leads. (Of course, this is not simply a principle of the 12 Steps. It's a commission given to every Christian: "Go out to all the world [including prisons] and tell the Good News.") (Matthew 28: 19-20)

I bring all this up because of the deep and complex difficulties now surrounding a ministry dear to my heart: the Kairos work we are doing at Menard in southern Illinois. It would take me the better part of a day to explain those difficulties with any level of fairness or in a truly useful level of detail. And that's not really my point.

Rather, I simply want to ask that if this Lenten blog has touched your spirit in some small way, you would now consider giving that gift away, in the form of a prayer for the entire community at Menard: The Warden and staff; the chaplains; the correctional officers; the inmates; and particularly the inmates (my Kairos brothers) who have themselves had a spiritual awakening as the result of our encounters there.

I know myself how very difficult it can be to keep the spiritual fires burning. I rely on community (my sisters and brothers in Christ) to remind me of God's faithfulness, to reassure me of God's power. I am deeply blessed to have all of you in my life, showing me the face of Christ, especially in those times of weariness or despair. I cannot imagine a vibrant faith life *without* you, without the benefit of the 12th Step.

Yet that is precisely the condition in which our Kairos brothers often find themselves at Menard. The difficulties there make it hard, if not impossible, for them to meet with each other on a regular basis. They cannot always lift each other up. And those of us in the Kairos community "outside" are often prevented by circumstances from returning there, to help stir the spiritual embers into flame once again.

So what *can* we do, but pray? In your charity, please pray for them today, perhaps through these words from Psalm 69:

> *See, you lowly ones, and be glad;*
> *You who seek God, may your hearts revive!*
> *For the Lord hears the poor,*
> *And his own who are in bonds he spurns not.*

AN UPDATE – in gratitude to all you Prayer Warriors:

Yesterday, many of the Kairos volunteers were in Chester, Illinois, attending an appreciation luncheon, sponsored by the chaplain at Menard. The event was held at the medium-security prison nearby, and when the conversation turned to the spring 2013 retreat (in grave danger of being cancelled), someone asked if the weekend could be held next month at the medium-security prison instead.

Well, I'm delighted to report that the answer was *"yes!"* It was an amazing thing to hear, because typically such decisions don't come anywhere nearly that quickly in prison ministry. It is a miracle of sorts – proof (to me, at least) that prayer works!

– 888 –

Scripture, to pray and ponder:

But I said, "I've worked for nothing. I've nothing to show for a life of hard work. Nevertheless, I'll let God have the last word.

Isaiah 49: 4

Day 42

Today's find: A pilgrim's progress

My heart is full on this final day of Lent. I am overwhelmed by the abundance of "found" spiritual gifts that have been showered on me over the past six weeks. I am humbled, too, by the outpouring of support (both "real" and "virtual") I have received because of this blog.

When I set out on Ash Wednesday, I noted that due to some particular areas of sinfulness in my life, I had been dreading the start of this holy season.

Now, seen in the rear-view mirror, I realize that it has instead been a time of incredible blessings: a bounty far greater than I ever could have imagined.

Toward the end of his career, the great St. Louis broadcaster Jack Buck was fond of saying, "Lord, why have you been so good to me?" In some respects, I can imagine another man named Simon Peter saying much the same thing.

And here I am, on the last day of this year's Lenten pilgrimage, echoing their sentiments:

> *"You are too good to me, dear Lord. I have done nothing to deserve your constancy, your affection, your faithfulness, your love, your joy, your forgiveness, your*

> *encouragement, your daily whispers of inspiration. Yet, there it is, all that and more – a heaping mound of spiritual gifts, piled up at my doorstep.*
>
> *So thank you, Lord, for entrusting them to me. Thank you for the steadfast spirit you have renewed in me. And help me, Lord, to be a good and faithful steward over these gifts."*

Ah, yes: Stewardship. That's the *other* thing tugging at my heart today. From the start, I have believed this blog to be a "Lenten season" kind of deal. In fact, it's sort of a promise I made to many of you, when I invited you to read along: *"Once Easter arrives, this blog goes into 'archive' mode – no more updates!"*

So, then, what am I to do with the gift that "found spirituality" has become in my life?

On some level, I think it's important that I keep the promise about ending (and archiving) *Steadfast Spirit*. It has been good for me to have made this journey. It is also necessary, I think, that I do not cling to the experience. Like Mary Magdalene encountering the risen Christ on Easter morning, I am being stirred to let it go – and perhaps, to let new possibilities emerge in its place. (John 20: 16-17)

What does that mean, precisely? At the moment, I can't really say. My ears and my heart are open, if the Holy Spirit sends additional nuggets my way during our celebration of Triduum over the next several days.

And after Easter, we'll just have to see. But whatever emerges, I'll make it a point to spread the word to those who might be interested, via some sort of "final posting" to *Steadfast Spirit.* Until then, let me say thanks again for all the many ways in which you have blessed me, my sisters and brothers in Christ, throughout this holy season.

May the grace of the Lord Jesus be with you all!

– δδδ –

Scripture, to pray and ponder:

God has given me a well-taught tongue, so I know how to encourage tired people. [God] wakes me up in the morning, wakes me up, opens my ears to listen as one ready to take orders.

Isaiah 50: 4

Entering a New Season
Triduum & Easter
Reflections

Holy Thursday

Today's find: All in

Sometimes I can be pretty thick-headed, a tick slow on the uptake.

For example, I remember a light bulb coming on a few years back while I was reading Beatrice Bruteau's *Radical Optimism.*[69] Her topic was how to model Christ, in living an incarnational life. But she used an image that stopped me in my tracks: "Eventually, we will find," she wrote, "that we are lying in a manger as food for the world."

Before that moment, it had never occurred to me that this is precisely what a manger is: a *feeding* trough. Jesus' very first home, beyond Mary's womb, in our world.

Seen in the light of the gift that Christ would eventually make of himself in the Eucharist, it doesn't appear to be an accident, this humble beginning to his time on earth.

Today, of course, Eucharist is on my mind because it's Holy Thursday – the day we formally recall the "institution of the Eucharist." And far too often, I

---

[69] Learn more about Bruteau here: http://bit.ly/2CDVL74
And her 1993 book, here: http://bit.ly/2QdlfQx

think, we use two-dollar terms like that without allowing enough time for a light bulb to go on over our heads.

It helps me to *connect* the two images – the infant Jesus, lying in feeding trough…and the Eucharistic Jesus, lying in the palm of my hand, just before I consume him. When I take the time to do that, to make the connection, it always overwhelms me to consider how *vulnerable* the Lord is in both circumstances. He doesn't summon cosmic power to make a grand entrance. Instead, the Lord of the Cosmos is content to lie more or less *helpless* in our hands. He's "all in," as they say at the poker table. He believes that much in us.

The other memorable vignette we celebrate tonight is the washing of the feet. I've heard it described as a Eucharistic image, too: the evangelist John's take on the bread and the cup that we read about in the other three gospels. Here again, the symbolism is powerful and rich. Christ, the Master, is "all in": He will do *anything* for us, even stoop to wash our feet. Even open his arms on the cross.

But there's an intriguing twist to this episode: It requires a particular response from believers. Saint Peter did the honors for us at the Last Supper – the apostolic prototype for modern day parishioners: "You will *never* wash MY feet!!!" (John 13: 8)

Eventually, though, Peter relents. He himself finds the grace to go "all in" with Christ: "Not just my feet, but my hands and head as well."

Of course, we know that within a few hours, Peter's resolve has already weakened. But perhaps there's another Holy Thursday lesson in his stumbles: Christ will bless our decision to go all in with him. Christ will be there, always, to catch us when we fall. And then (as now) Christ promises to *feed* us, giving us the strength we need to carry on.

– δδδ –

Scripture, to pray and ponder:

Let me go over with you again exactly what goes on in the Lord's Supper and why it is so centrally important. I received my instructions from [Jesus] himself and passed them on to you…Jesus, on the night of his betrayal, took bread. Having given thanks, he broke it and said, "This is my body, broken for you. Do this to remember me."

1 Corinthians 11: 23-24

Good Friday

Today's find: Hidden treasure

On Good Friday, the Jesuits of Great Britain[70] invite us to consider Jesus, on the cross, his divinity hidden from our eyes.

As I listened to the reflection, I realized that I found this chosen "hiddenness" deeply troubling. *O Saving Victim, why did you find it necessary to* conceal *your power and glory from us – if even only for a few hours as you hung on the cross?*

Why did you conceal it – not just from *us* – but from the human beings you cherished *most* in this life? Why did you hide your impending victory over death from your own mother, and from the disciple whom you loved? Why, in your goodness, could you not find a way to keep their hearts from breaking?

Why, O Lord? Why?

And the more I wrestled with the question, the more I realized just how disturbing that word *why* can be.

In a sense, it is at the very heart of our broken spiritual condition as human beings. In times of pain or suffering, we *always* want to know why. We cannot

---

[70] This daily reflection site is always worth a listen: http://bit.ly/2JXkzuT

suppress the hiss of the serpent in our ear: "Eat of *this* fruit and you will be just like Gods…" (Genesis 3: 5)

Even though we are God's children, it is so very hard for us to believe that God has only good things in mind for us, that it *all* belongs, that "all things work together for good." (Romans 8: 28)

And so, while on the cross, Jesus hides his divinity from us, as if to give us one last (and very crucial) lesson about our relationship with God: "Father, into *your* hands I commend my spirit…" (Luke 23: 46)

Jesus says to his mother, and to the disciple(s) whom he loves: "Trust God."

"Lose your need to know every answer. Lose your very *self*, alongside Me, through the very crosses you bear."

"Change your heart. Master this movement in your life, and soon you will be with me in paradise." (Luke 23: 43)

– δδδ –

Scripture, to pray and ponder:

Like a lamb taken to be slaughtered and like a sheep being sheared, he took it all in silence.

Isaiah 53: 7

Holy Saturday

Today's find: Empty and beautiful, empty and inviting

I love the way the church building at my parish looks on Holy Saturday morning.

It's the same – but different – as any other day of the year. Pews and hymnals. Altar and ambo. Look off just to the right in the sanctuary, though, and you notice the tabernacle, bereft of its precious contents. Its doors are flung open. Its interior, usually hidden, now plain for all to see.

The emptiness is beautiful, inviting. It looks a bit like a tomb, one whose doors could not contain the Mystery within.

Get there early enough, and the church is quiet, too. It's a great chance to share a moment with the Lord, in joyful hope and thanksgiving.

Morning prayer begins at 8:30, another shift from the usual routine. Antiphonal prayer, rather than Mass. And it feeds our spirits, both the "regulars" who are realizing how much they miss their daily connection with the Eucharist, and the catechumens, candidates and sponsors all gathered in anticipation of their entry into the Mystery at the Vigil.

I welcome the peacefulness, the break from the routine. I am grateful for the solitude, as long as it lasts. I am touched by the energy, too: the Word, stirring into life in the hearts of the "newbies" – a miracle of conversion taking place right before my very eyes.

The church building, on Holy Saturday morning, is definitely a place where *less* is *more*. Liturgical trappings have been stripped away. And yet, Jesus is there, beckoning all the same.

Come, sit with me, he says. (John 13: 23) Recline at my side. Enjoy my presence. Notice what is missing *from this scene. And notice, too, how I am still very much here with you, in this place, at this moment.*

A few years back, I remember reading about what the cosmologists call Dark Matter – the unseen "stuff" that comprises more than 90% of the material in the universe.[71] "We know it exists," the astrophysicists will tell you. "But the only way we can identify it is by its effects on known objects."

"Dark Matter?" Frankly, I think they've got the name all wrong. Whether we are peering into space through a radio telescope, or peering into an empty tabernacle on Holy Saturday morning, we are being invited to

---

[71] Read up on "dark matter" here: http://bit.ly/2NI6hAD

catch a glimpse of what, otherwise, we are too blind to see.

We wait there, holding the Mystery in our hearts, anticipating the Joy that is to come.

– δδδ –

Scripture, to pray and ponder:

God looked over everything he had made; it was so good, so very good! It was evening, it was morning – Day Six.

Genesis 1: 31

Easter Sunday

Today's find: Paschal people

Admittedly, I haven't had much of chance to get to know the new Pope, but he's already starting to grow on me. He seems like "Easter people."

In the Gospels, we meet quite a cast from that first Easter:

- The women from Galilee (*Luke* names three: Mary Magdalene, Joanna, Mary the mother of James; *Matthew*, two: Mary Magdalene and the other Mary; *Mark* adds the curious detail that out of Magdalene, Jesus had driven seven demons; she is the only woman named in *John's* account.)
- Peter – always running, but never seeming to get anywhere. (John 20: 4)
- The rest of the apostles – to whom "the story seemed like nonsense," according to Luke.
- The disciples on the road to Emmaus, unable to recognize the Master walking right alongside them. (Luke 24: 13-35)

Upon close inspection, the original Easter people look like anything *but* saints. They seem dazed and confused. They are filled with doubt. And what instincts they *do* follow don't seem to be at all what the resurrected Jesus has in mind. Imagine how it must have pierced Mary Magdalene's heart when Jesus upbraided her for the hug she so desperately wanted to give him. (John 20: 17)

But here's the thing about Easter people: They don't let the story end there, whether it's in doubt or amazement. Somehow, they know that what they have just witnessed is not simply a magic trick. It's not even just another one of Jesus' mighty deeds. And they allow it to *change* them. They allow *Him* – the risen Lord – to change them, even though none really has any idea what it will mean.

It's a trait they appear to have in common with Pope Francis. I'll always cherish the first image I saw of him, stepping out onto the balcony to extend a blessing to the throng below in St. Peter's Square. He, too, looked dazed and confused – a fisherman who couldn't seem to remember where he docked his boat. I was touched by his humanity in that moment. Touched by his *courage*, as well, in accepting a job that he clearly didn't aspire to.

And then I read about one of his initial papal tweets. *"Being with Jesus demands that we go out from ourselves, and from living a tired and habitual faith."*

What a concept for us to contemplate as we celebrate this great feast. Pope Francis reminds us that Easter people don't cling to the past. Easter people resist the temptation to say, "been there, done that." Easter people always step forward in faith.

Easter people embrace vitality over comfort – because they (we) have seen the risen Lord…and we simply can't get enough of Him!

— δδδ —

Scripture, to pray and ponder:

Yeast, too, is a "small thing," but it works its way through a whole batch of bread dough pretty fast. So get rid of this "[old] yeast." Our true identity is flat and plain, not puffed up with the wrong kind of ingredient.

1 Corinthians 5: 6-7

Mystagogia[72]

Today's find: Omega…and Alpha

Omega: As I mentioned on the last day of Lent, *Steadfast Spirit* has been an incredible blessing in my life. But the time has come to call it a wrap, so this will be the final "reflection" post I make to this blog (although I intend to keep the archive available, if that's of interest to you).

Alpha: And with the new life of Easter, something is beginning in me, too. I'm not entirely sure what that means, or how it will play out. At least for now, the next step is a new blog of "found spirituality" – called *With Us Still*.[73]

I invite you to follow along, even though I don't know exactly what I'm inviting you to. More like a *regular* blog than a *daily* blog, perhaps? Of course, the Holy Spirit may have other ideas entirely. But I'm game, if you are.

---

[72] 'Mystagogia' is all about what happens after the Lenten and Easter journey: http://bit.ly/2qO2Yyy

[73] Surprisingly (to me, anyway), I'm still blogging about "found" spirituality six years later. Here's where to catch up, if you are so inclined: https://withusstill.blog/

About the author

Having now composed more than 500 blog posts of "found" spirituality, John Schroeder remains fond of the first 50 or so he ever wrote. The entries presented in this volume opened the door for John to consider a new way of writing following on his successful 35-year career as business freelancer serving corporate and non-profit clients. John and his wife Gerri, both graduates of Saint Louis University, recently celebrated their 40th anniversary in the glad company of their three children, two spouses, and three grandchildren.